W9-ATB-542

PRIMER OF
LABOR RELATIONS

24th Edition

PRIMER OF
LABOR RELATIONS

24th Edition

John J. Kenny
Assistant Managing Editor
Labor Relations Reporter

Linda G. Kahn
Legal Editor
Labor Relations Reporter

The Bureau of National Affairs, Inc., Washington, D.C.

Copyright © 1947, 1953, 1961, 1964, 1966,
1967, 1969, 1971, 1973, 1975, 1980, 1983, 1986, 1989
The Bureau of National Affairs, Inc.

Authorization to photocopy items for internal or
personal use, or the internal or personal use of
specific clients, is granted by BNA Books for
libraries and other users registered with the
Copyright Clearance Center (CCC) Transactional
Reporting Service, provided that $0.50 per page
is paid directly to CCC, 21 Congress St., Salem,
MA 01970.   0-87179-617-1/89/$0 + .50

Published by BNA Books
1231 25th St., NW, Washington, D.C. 20037

Library of Congress Catalog Number: 56-2617
International Standard Serial Number: 0272-0574
International Standard Book Number: 0-87179-617-1

Printed in the United States of America

PREFACE

This brief book summarizes the law of labor relations in the United States as it exists today. The evolution of this law began with the passage of the Wagner Act (or National Labor Relations Act) in 1935, which established the principle that employees have the right to organize into labor unions and to bargain collectively with their employers.

Twelve years later the outbreak of strikes and general labor unrest at the end of World War II led Congress to conclude that the labor law was weighted too heavily in favor of unions. This resulted in the adoption in 1947 of the Taft-Hartley Act (or Labor Management Relations Act), which amended the Wagner Act to add protections for employees and employers.

Another 12 years elapsed before the next major change in the basic labor law. This occurred in 1959 with the passage of the Landrum-Griffin Act, which was triggered by the investigations of the McClellan Committee into alleged racketeering and abuses of members' rights by certain labor unions.

Thus, our basic law of labor relations today stems from the Wagner Act as amended by the Taft-Hartley and Landrum-Griffin Acts. It is mostly commonly referred to as either the Taft-Hartley Act (or Taft Act) or the Labor Management Relations Act (LMRA). This law, as interpreted by the National Labor Relations Board (NLRB) and the federal and state courts, is the main focus of this book.

Title VII of the Civil Rights Act of 1964, another major law of employee relations, sets forth the ground rules for equal employment opportunity. This law is dealt with in a separate *Primer of Equal Employment Opportunity*. Various laws that govern wages and hours, including the Fair Labor Standards Act, are discussed in detail in the *Primer on Wage & Hour Laws*. Both primers are published by BNA Books.

This edition covers relevant cases decided through 1988. Readers should consult current issues of the *Labor Relations Reporter* for the most recent developments in the law.

Citations for cases mentioned by name in the course of the discussion are contained in the Table of Cases following the Glossary of Labor Terms. References in the Table of Cases are to official reporters, when available, and to BNA publications, including the *Labor Relations Reference Manual (LRRM)* and *Fair Employment Practice Cases* (FEP Cases).

Throughout the book, statutes are referred to as published in BNA's *Labor Relations Expediter* (LRX). When the term Labor Board or merely Board is used without further qualification, it refers to the National Labor Relations Board. The abbreviation EEOC refers to the Equal Employment Opportunity Commission.

CONTENTS

1

THE LAW OF LABOR RELATIONS—A BIRD'S-EYE VIEW

The federal law governing labor relations rests on three basic statutes, the first adopted in 1935 and the other two at 12-year intervals thereafter. These laws—the Wagner, Taft-Hartley, and Landrum-Griffin Acts—provide the foundation for a complex structure of rules, regulations, and decisions.

THE WAGNER ACT

In adopting the Wagner Act or National Labor Relations Act in 1935, Congress established the principle that employees should be protected in their rights to organize into labor organizations and to bargain collectively concerning wages and working conditions. To provide this protection, the Act made it an unfair labor practice for an employer to do any of the following:

- Interfere with, restrain, or coerce employees in the exercise of their rights to organize, bargain collectively, and engage in other concerted activities for their mutual aid or protection.
- Dominate or interfere with the formation or administration of any labor organization or contribute financial or other support to it.

1

- Encourage or discourage membership in any labor organization by discrimination with regard to hiring or tenure or conditions of employment, subject to an exception for valid union-security agreements.
- Discharge or otherwise discriminate against an employee because he has filed charges or given testimony under the Act.
- Refuse to bargain collectively with the majority representative of his employees.

In addition to forbidding the five employer unfair labor practices, the Act set up election machinery to permit employees to choose collective bargaining representatives. The National Labor Relations Board was created to administer and enforce the Act.

THE TAFT-HARTLEY ACT

In the 12 years following the enactment of the Wagner Act, many members of Congress became convinced that the balance in labor-management relations had become too heavily weighted in favor of the unions. They believed that employers and employees needed protection against unfair practices of unions and that the public needed protection against labor disputes resulting in work stoppages that threatened the national health or safety.

The Taft-Hartley Act adopted in 1947 sought to provide such protection and restore the balance in labor relations. The new law was built upon the framework of the Wagner Act, retaining the provisions for exclusive representation of employees by majority bargaining agents and the restrictions on unfair labor practices of employers. But virtually all of the Wagner Act's major provisions were amended or qualified in some respect, and an entirely new code of conduct for unions and their agents was established.

In addition to the five employer unfair practices forbidden by the Wagner Act, the Taft-Hartley Act forbade a series of unfair labor practices by unions. It became unlawful for a union to do any of the following:

- Restrain or coerce employees in the exercise of their rights under the Act.
- Restrain or coerce an employer in the selection of his bargaining or grievance representative.
- Cause or attempt to cause an employer to discriminate against an employee on account of his membership or nonmembership in a labor organization, subject to an exception for valid union-shop agreements.
- Refuse to bargain collectively (in good faith) with an employer if the union has been designated as bargaining agent by a majority of the employees.
- Induce or encourage employees to stop work in order to force an employer or self-employed person to join a union or in order to force an employer or other person to stop doing business with any other person (secondary boycott).
- Induce or encourage employees to stop work in order to force an employer to recognize and bargain with the union where another union has been certified as bargaining agent (strike against a certification).
- Induce or encourage employees to stop work in order to force an employer to assign particular work to members of the union instead of to members of another union (jurisdictional strike).
- Charge an excessive or discriminatory fee as a condition to becoming a member of the union.
- Cause or attempt to cause an employer to pay for services that are not performed or not to be performed (featherbedding).

The Taft-Hartley Act also made some important changes in the rules for representation elections. The NLRB's discretion in determining appropriate units was limited, replaced economic strikers lost their voting rights, the Board was barred from conducting more than one election a year in a particular unit, and a number of other changes were made in the election machinery.

THE LANDRUM-GRIFFIN ACT

The adoption of the third basic federal labor law, the Labor-Management Reporting and Disclosure Act of 1959, was triggered by the disclosures of the McClellan Committee. In two and one-half years of investigation and public hearings, the Committee compiled an imposing record of wrongdoing on the part of certain unions and their officers, of coercion of employees and small employers, and of shady dealings and interference with employees' rights by "middlemen" serving as management consultants. The Act was aimed at eliminating these practices.

Essentially, the 1959 Act was two statutes. First, there was a code of conduct for unions, union officers, employers, and consultants. Second, there was a group of significant amendments to the Taft-Hartley Act, amendments that both modified existing provisions and added entirely new provisions.

The code of conduct guarantees certain inalienable rights to union members within their union and imposes certain obligations on unions, union officers, employers, and consultants. In brief, this is what the code does:

- Every labor organization is required to have a constitution and bylaws containing certain minimum standards and safeguards. Reports on the union's policies and procedures, as well as annual financial reports, must be filed with the Secretary of Labor and must be disclosed to the union's members.
- Union members have a bill of rights to protect their rights within the union.
- Standards are established for union trusteeships and union elections. Reports on trusteeships must be made to the Secretary of Labor.
- A fiduciary obligation is imposed on union officers, and they are required to file reports with the Secretary of Labor on conflict-of-interest transactions.
- Employers and labor relations consultants are required to file reports on expenditures and arrangements that affect employees' organizing and bargaining rights.
- The Secretary of Labor is made the watchdog of union conduct. He is the custodian of reports from unions and

their officers, and he is given the power to investigate and prosecute violations of many provisions of the Act.

THE 1959 TAFT-HARTLEY AMENDMENTS

The amendments to the Taft-Hartley Act included in the 1959 Reform or Landrum-Griffin Act were a blend of so-called labor sweeteners, sought by unions, and additional restrictions on unions' strike, picketing, and boycott weapons, sought by employers. But the additional restrictions appeared in some respects to have outweighed the labor sweeteners. In brief, here is what the amendments did:

- State courts and labor relations boards were given jurisdiction over cases rejected by the NLRB under its jurisdictional standards. This eliminated the "no-man's-land" created by the Supreme Court's *Guss* decision.
- Permanently replaced economic strikers were given the right to vote in representation elections conducted by the NLRB within one year after the beginning of the strike, subject to regulations to be issued by the NLRB.
- Three loopholes in the secondary boycott prohibition apparently were closed, and hot-cargo agreements were outlawed, subject to exceptions relating to subcontracting in the construction and garment industries.
- A new unfair labor practice made it unlawful for a union to picket for recognition or organizational purposes under certain circumstances.
- Pre-hire and seven-day union-shop contracts were legalized in the construction industry.

The Taft-Hartley Act, as amended, appears at LRX 3751; the Landrum-Griffin Act is at LRX 6501.

HOSPITAL AMENDMENT TO TAFT-HARTLEY ACT

In 1974, Congress passed an amendment extending the coverage of the Act to private nonprofit hospitals and nursing homes. The NLRB already had asserted jurisdiction over proprietary hospitals and nursing homes by decision.

The amendment provides for compulsory mediation of hospital disputes by the Federal Mediation and Conciliation Service. It also requires that a union give the FMCS and the hospital 10 days' notice before striking or picketing.

OTHER FEDERAL LABOR LAWS

There are a number of other important federal labor laws. Some preceded the National Labor Relations Act; others followed it. They deal with a wide range of subjects—e.g., railway labor disputes, labor injunctions, minimum wages, strikebreakers, labor racketeering, equal employment opportunity, and private pension plans. The following are capsule summaries of what these other laws do.

Age Discrimination

The Age Discrimination in Employment Act prohibits discrimination against workers between 40 and 70 years of age. It forbids employers of more than 20 persons to do any of the following:

- Discharge, fail or refuse to hire, or otherwise discriminate against any individual because of his age with respect to compensation, terms, conditions, or privileges of employment.
- Limit, segregate, or classify an employee in any way that would deprive him of job opportunities or adversely affect his employment because of his age.
- Reduce the wage rate of an employee in order to comply with the Act.
- Indicate any preference, limitation, specification, or discrimination based on age in any notices or advertisements for employment.
- Operate a seniority system or employee benefit plan that requires or permits the involuntary retirement of an employee under age 70. There are limited exceptions dealing with the retirement of top business executives.

These prohibitions do not apply where age is a bona fide occupational qualification, or where a differentiation is based on reasonable factors other than age.

The Act also applies to employment agencies serving covered employers and to labor unions with 25 or more members. Employment agencies are forbidden to fail or refuse to refer individuals for employment because of age. Unions are forbidden to expel or exclude persons from membership on the basis of age.

The Act was amended in 1974 to cover federal and state employees. In 1978, the Act was amended to eliminate the maximum retirement age of 70 formerly in effect for federal employees. The Act was amended in 1984 to cover U.S. citizens working overseas.

The text of the Age Discrimination in Employment Act appears at LRX 1823.

Antiracketeering Act

The Hobbs Antiracketeering Act of 1946 (LRX 6803) forbids criminal conspiracy to impede interstate commerce by extortion or robbery. As adopted in 1934, the Act exempted "the payment of wages by a bona fide employer to a bona fide employee." The Supreme Court in 1942 construed this exemption to protect a member of a truckers' union against prosecution for stopping trucks operated by nonunion employees and compelling them to pay sums of money equivalent to the union pay scale. *(United States v. Teamsters Local 807)* The Act was amended by Congress in 1946 to delete the exemption. Violators are subject to criminal penalties.

Antistrikebreaking Act

The Byrnes Antistrikebreaking Act of 1938 (LRX 4401) forbids the interstate transportation of persons to be used to interfere with peaceful picketing in a labor dispute or with the processes of collective bargaining.

Civil Rights Acts

Title VII of the Civil Rights Act of 1964 makes it unlawful for employers, labor unions, and employment agencies in industries affecting interstate commerce to discriminate in employment or union membership against any individual because of his race, color, religion, sex, or national origin. The provisions of Title VII are administered by the Equal Employment Opportunity Commission. Prior to April 24, 1972, the Commission was limited to seeking compliance through a system of formal and informal remedial procedures, including conference, conciliation, and persuasion. But it could not bring an action in court against an employer, union, or employment agency alleged to have violated the Act. Aggrieved employees, however, could sue upon a finding by the Commission of reasonable cause to believe a violation had been committed—a requirement construed liberally by the courts to permit aggrieved individuals to assert their rights where the Commission delayed in processing a charge. The Justice Department also was authorized to bring an action where it found an alleged "pattern or practice" of violation.

On April 24, 1972, President Nixon signed the Equal Employment Opportunity Act of 1972, authorizing the Commission to bring an action in a federal district court where it found reasonable cause to believe a violation had been committed. If the Commission failed to sue, the aggrieved individuals could bring an action themselves. Jurisdiction to bring "pattern or practice" actions was to be shared with the Department of Justice for two years; thereafter the Commission would have exclusive jurisdiction over such actions.

The 1972 Act also extended the coverage of Title VII. The most important change was that which made state and local governments subject to the prohibitions.

Title VII was amended in 1978 to provide that discrimination on the basis of sex includes discrimination based on "pregnancy, childbirth or related medical conditions."

The text of Title VII appears at LRX 1801.

The field of employment discrimination also is regulated by:

- The Civil Rights Act of 1866 (42 U.S.C. § 1981), which gives all persons the same contractual rights as "white citizens."
- The Civil Rights Act of 1871 (42 U.S.C. § 1983), which applies to persons acting "under color of state law" to deprive others of federal rights.
- The Equal Pay Act of 1963, which makes it unlawful to pay a lower wage to members of the opposite sex for equal work on jobs that require equal skill, effort, and responsibility under similar working conditions in the same establishment.
- Executive Orders 11246 and 11141, which forbid employment discrimination based on race, color, religion, sex, national origin, or age by companies with federal contracts exceeding $10,000. A company with 50 or more employees and a government contract for $50,000 or more must develop a written affirmative action plan.
- The Vocational Rehabilitation Act of 1973, which requires employers with federal contracts over $2,500 to take affirmative action for the employment of the handicapped. If the company has 50 or more employees and its contract is for $50,000 or more, it must prepare a written affirmative action program. The Act defines a handicapped individual as a person who has—or who is regarded as having—a "physical or mental impairment which substantially limits one or more of such person's major life activities."

Other laws applicable in the equal employment opportunity area include Title VI of the Civil Rights Act of 1964, Title IX of the Education Amendments of 1972, the Civil Rights Attorney's Fees Awards Act of 1976, the Vietnam Era Veterans Readjustment Assistance Act, and the State and Local Fiscal Assistance Act of 1972.

Norris-LaGuardia Act

Adopted in 1932 to prevent abuse of injunctions in labor disputes, the Norris-LaGuardia Anti-Injunction Act (LRX 3501) forbids the federal courts to issue injunctions in labor disputes except under strictly limited conditions. Before an injunction may be issued, it must be shown, among other things, that there were prior efforts to settle the dispute peaceably, that law enforcement officials are unable or unwilling to safeguard the employer's property, and that a denial of an injunction will entail greater loss to the employer than granting it will cause to the union. No injunctions may be issued against peaceful picketing. The Act also outlawed the "yellow dog" contract under which a worker, as a condition of employment, agrees not to join or remain a member of a union.

The Taft-Hartley and Landrum-Griffin Acts made some exceptions to the Norris-LaGuardia Act.

Occupational Safety and Health Act

In 1970, Congress adopted the Occupational Safety and Health Act—one of the most comprehensive laws affecting labor-management relations. Its coverage extends to all employees whose activities affect interstate commerce. Basically, it requires employers and employees to comply with safety and health standards promulgated by the Labor Department. There are stringent penalties for violations.

Racketeer Influenced and Corrupt Organizations Act

The RICO Act prohibits anyone who has received income from a pattern of racketeering from using such income to establish any enterprise that affects commerce. It is also unlawful for any person "through a pattern of racketeering activity" to acquire or maintain any interest in an enterprise that affects commerce. The Act also prohibits any person from conducting the affairs of an enterprise through a pattern of racketeering activity or collection of unlawful debt. Racketeering activity includes, among many other things, any act that is indictable under the Hobbs Act or under sections of the Taft-Hartley Act dealing with restrictions on payments and loans to unions and embezzlement from union funds.

The RICO Act has been found applicable in cases where a union used violent tactics to conduct a recognitional strike *(Yellow Bus Lines v. Teamsters Local 639)* and where members of a union's executive board and other individuals extorted union membership rights guaranteed by the Landrum-Griffin Act. *(United States v. Teamsters Local 560)*

Railway Labor Act

Adopted in 1926, this law provides a means of naming bargaining agents for employees of carriers through elections conducted by the National Mediation Board. It also provides some dispute settlement and arbitration procedures. In brief, these procedures are as follows:

- Disputes over the interpretation or application of collective bargaining contracts in the railroad industry that are not resolved by the parties may be referred by either party to the National Railroad Adjustment Board. Although recourse to the Adjustment Board is voluntary, an award made by the Board is enforceable in court. The 1966 amendments also provided for limited judicial review of awards on suit by either party.

- A railroad or union desiring to make a change in wages, rules, or working conditions must give at least 30-days' written notice. If the proposed change results in a dispute, either party may request the services of the National Mediation Board or the Board may proffer its services if it finds that a labor emergency exists. If the Board fails to resolve the dispute by mediation, it then must try to induce the parties to submit the dispute to binding arbitration.

- When all of these procedures fail and a strike is threatened, the President is authorized to appoint an emergency board to investigate and report to the President concerning the dispute within 30 days after it is created. Until the emergency board reports and for 30 days thereafter, strikes and lockouts are forbidden, although no penalty is provided for violating the ban.

In 1936, all provisions of the Act except those relating to the Adjustment Board were made applicable to air carriers and their employees. Instead of a national adjustment board, each air carrier and the representatives of its employees must establish a system board of adjustment to resolve disputes as to the meaning and application of their contracts.

The Railway Labor Act appears at LRX 6001.

Wage-Hour Laws

There are a number of federal laws setting wage-hour standards for employees engaged in interstate commerce or government contract work. The Fair Labor Standards Act (LRX 8101) establishes minimum wage, overtime, and child labor standards for employees engaged in interstate commerce or the production of goods for interstate commerce. The Walsh-Healey Act (LRX 8301) establishes similar standards for employees working on government supply contracts. The Davis-Bacon, Contract Work Hours Standards, and Copeland Antikickback Acts (LRX 8001, 8071, 8051) establish minimum wage, fringe benefit, and overtime standards for employees working on government-financed construction projects. The Fair Labor Standards Act was amended in 1963 to forbid wage differentials based solely on sex, effective in June 1964.

The Service Contracts Act of 1965 (LRX 8081) requires employers performing service contracts for government agencies to pay their employees not less than the minimum wages and fringe benefits found by the Secretary of Labor to be prevailing locally. In no event may they pay their employees less than the minimum wage under the Fair Labor Standards Act.

Welfare Fund Disclosure

The Welfare and Pension Plans Disclosure Act adopted by Congress in 1958 requires administrators of employee welfare and pension plans to make detailed reports to participants and the Secretary of Labor. The reports must disclose the terms of the plans and their financial operations. In 1962, the Act was amended to give the Secretary of Labor interpretative, investigative, and enforcement powers. Kickbacks, embezzlement, conflicts of interest, and false entries by fund officials or employees were made federal crimes subject to stiff penalties. The Employee Retirement Income Security Act, adopted in 1974, established additional fiduciary standards for plan administrators. It also provided for mandatory vesting of benefits and funding of plans. An agency was established to insure benefits in the event of the termination of a plan.

THE STATE LABOR LAWS

A substantial proportion of the states also have laws relating to the conduct of labor-management relations or the activities of labor unions. Some preceded the federal statutes; others followed the adoption of the federal laws and were patterned after them. A number of states, for example, have little Norris-LaGuardia acts limiting the jurisdiction of state courts to issue injunctions in labor disputes. Others have little Wagner or Taft-Hartley acts. There also are the state fair employment practice laws, right-to-work laws forbidding all forms of union-security contracts, and laws restricting the rights of unions to strike or picket, although many of the restrictions on strikes or picketing have been invalidated by judicial holdings.

The states have long followed the common-law doctrine of employment at will, under which an employee hired for an indefinite term may be discharged for any reason, absent contractual or statutory limitation. *(Payne v. A.R.R. Co.)* But courts are now recognizing exceptions to this doctrine, the principal ones being for discharges that are found to violate public policy or to breach an implied contract. *(Novosel v. Nationwide Insurance Co., Toussaint v. Blue Cross)*

A discussion of the employment-at-will doctrine and other individual employment issues appears at LRX 560:101.

PREEMPTION DOCTRINE

Whenever a state law covers an area also regulated by a federal statute, problems of exclusive or concurrent jurisdiction and federal preemption arise. The 1959 amendment to the

Taft-Hartley Act, giving the states authority to handle cases rejected by the NLRB under its jurisdictional standards, resolved one of the most difficult of these problems.

The Supreme Court has articulated three major types of preemption analysis under the Taft-Hartley Act. The first protects the primary jurisdiction of the NLRB by preempting claims involving conduct that is arguably protected or prohibited by the Act. The second type encompasses conduct that is not arguably protected or prohibited by the Act, but which Congress intended to be left unregulated so it could be "controlled by the free play of economic forces." The third type of preemption arises in the context of state law claims that concern conduct covered by the terms of a collective bargaining contract.

The Supreme Court's decisions in preemption cases are often complicated, and various exceptions have developed. Supreme Court rulings on preemption include the following:

- When an activity is arguably prohibited or protected by the Taft-Hartley Act, the states and federal courts must defer to the exclusive competence of the NLRB. *(San Diego Building & Constr. Trades Council v. Garmon)*
- An employee's state court breach of contract action against his union was preempted because the union's conduct in obtaining the employee's discharge arguably violated the Taft-Hartley Act. *(Motor Coach Employees v. Lockridge)*
- A state law action against a union and its officers seeking damages for defamatory statements by union adherents published during an organizing campaign was not preempted by the Taft-Hartley Act. The state was found to have an overriding concern in the control of malicious libel. *(Linn v. United Plant Guard Workers)*
- A union's concerted refusal to work overtime, which was intended to put pressure on an employer to renew its collective bargaining contract, was peaceful conduct constituting activity that must be free of state regulation, and thus a state labor board improperly enjoined such activity. *(Machinists Lodge 76 v. Wisconsin Employment Relations Commission)*

- The fact that a union's trespassory picketing of an employer's store was arguably protected by the Taft-Hartley Act did not deprive a state court of jurisdiction over the employer's trespass claim. Because the assertion of state jurisdiction did not create a significant risk of prohibition of protected conduct, the Court was unwilling to presume that Congress intended the arguably protected character of the union's conduct to deprive the state court of jurisdiction. *(Sears, Roebuck & Co. v. San Diego County District Council of Carpenters)*

- The New Jersey Casino Control Act was not preempted by the Taft-Hartley Act to the extent that the state statute imposed limitations on whom casino industry employees can choose to serve as officials of their bargaining representatives. *(Brown v. Hotel & Restaurant Employees Local 54)*

- A state court action brought by a discharged supervisor against a union for interference with his employment relations was preempted. The question whether the discharge was the result of union influence was present in both the unfair labor practice case and the state law claim. *(Operating Engineers Local 926 v. Jones)*

- A Wisconsin statute that barred from doing business with the state those persons or firms who had repeatedly violated the Taft-Hartley Act was preempted. The state debarment law was found to function as a supplemental sanction for violations of the Taft-Hartley Act. *(Wisconsin Department of Industry, Labor and Human Relations v. Gould, Inc.)*

- State law misrepresentation and breach of contract claims brought against an employer by strike replacements, who were displaced by reinstated strikers after they had been promised permanent jobs, were not preempted. The state has a substantial interest in protecting its citizens from misrepresentations that have caused them grievous harm, the Court said. *(Belknap, Inc. v. Hale)*

- A city's action in conditioning a taxicab franchise renewal on the settlement of an employer's labor dispute with a union was preempted by the Taft-Hartley Act. The settlement conditions imposed by the city destroyed the balance of power in labor disputes designed by Congress and frustrated Congress' decision to leave open the use of economic weapons. *(Golden State Transit Corp. v. City of Los Angeles)*

- An employee's state law tort action alleging bad-faith delay in making disability-benefit payments due under a collective bargaining contract was preempted. "When resolution of a state-law claim is substantially dependent upon analysis of the terms of an agreement made between the parties in a labor contract," it must be either treated as a claim under the Taft-Hartley Act or dismissed as preempted by federal labor-contract law. *(Allis-Chalmers Corp. v. Lueck)*
- A state law tort claim that a union breached its duty to provide a member with a safe workplace depends substantially on interpretation of a collective bargaining contract and therefore is preempted by the Taft-Hartley Act. *(Electrical Workers (IBEW) v. Hechler)*
- A state law retaliatory discharge claim brought by an injured employee who was discharged after she requested workmen's compensation was not preempted by the Taft-Hartley Act, even though the employee was covered by a collective bargaining contract that protected her from being fired without just cause. The state-law claim involves purely factual questions pertaining to the conduct of the employee and the conduct and motivation of the employer and does not require construing the meaning of the contract, the Court said. *(Lingle v. Norge Division of Magic Chef, Inc.)*

2
WHO IS COVERED
BY THE LAW

Whether a particular worker, union, or employer is covered by the provisions of the Taft-Hartley Act depends on the statutory definitions of the terms "interstate commerce," "employer," and "employee." But even if a worker qualifies as an "employee" and his employer's activities are such as to bring him within the coverage of the Act, the employee still may not be able to get his case before the NLRB. The NLRB limits the cases it will accept by use of a series of jurisdictional standards. These standards are based on the dollar volume of goods the employer buys from or ships to other states or the annual dollar volume of business he does.

TEST OF "AFFECTING COMMERCE"

It was the intention of Congress to extend the application of the Act to the farthest reaches of interstate commerce. The test is whether the employer's activities "affect" interstate commerce. Except in the District of Columbia, where all commerce is covered, the commerce "affected" must be such type as crosses state lines.

But this does not mean that products must be shipped across state lines. It is sufficient that raw materials, power, or communications used cross state lines. Potentially, therefore,

17

the NLRB is given the authority to exercise its jurisdiction over all but the smallest of businesses.

The NLRB, however, has never exercised its broad statutory grant of jurisdiction to the fullest. It has used its administrative discretion to fix limits beyond which it will not tread. Since 1950, it has done this by application of a set of jurisdictional yardsticks.

In 1958, the Board revised these standards in such a way as to lay the basis for the broadest assertion of jurisdiction it ever had exercised. For a manufacturing company, for example, the test was $50,000 annual receipts from or shipments to other states. For retail firms, the test was $500,000 gross annual volume of business. Moreover, the 1959 amendments to the law forbid the Board to ever change the standards in such a way as to reduce the number of cases it will accept. See LRX 610:203 for the standards for the various categories of business.

Congress expanded the jurisdiction of the NLRB in 1970 to include labor relations in the U.S. Postal Service—except to the extent inconsistent with other provisions of the Postal Reorganization Act—and in 1974 to include private hospitals and nursing homes. The NLRB itself has expanded its jurisdiction over the years—asserting jurisdiction, for example, over private colleges and universities *(Cornell University, NLRB Rule making power under APA)*, charitable institutions *(St. Aloysious Home)*, day-care centers *(Salt & Pepper Nursery School)*, law firms *(Foley, Hoag & Eliot, Wayne County Legal Services)*, job-corps centers *(Singer Co.)*, and hotels and motels, whether residential or non-residential. *(Penn-Keystone Realty Corp.)* It has also asserted jurisdiction over sheltered workshops, but one appeals court has disagreed. *(NLRB v. Lighthouse for the Blind, Arkansas Lighthouse for the Blind v. NLRB)*

RELIGIOUSLY SPONSORED ORGANIZATIONS

Teachers in schools operated by a church to teach both religious and secular subjects were not within the NLRB's jurisdiction, the Supreme Court ruled. It rejected the Board's contention that jurisdiction over religiously sponsored organizations should be declined only when the organizations are completely religious, not just religiously associated. *(NLRB v. Catholic Bishop of Chicago)*

The Board interprets the *Catholic Bishop* decision as applying to colleges and universities, not just to elementary and secondary schools. *(Trustee of St. Joseph's College)*

Relying on *Catholic Bishop*, the Board declined to assert jurisdiction over a church-related school, whose purpose, in substantial part, was to propagate religious faith. *(Jewish Day School)* But the Board did assert jurisdiction over a church-supported college, finding that the purpose of the college was secular and that the teachers were not required to submit to or support the bishops or teachings of the church. *(Livingstone College)*

WHO IS AN "EMPLOYEE"

The Act's definition of an "employee" includes not only persons currently on an employer's payroll but also persons whose work has ceased because of a current strike or an unfair labor practice and who have not obtained other regular and substantially equivalent employment. The following workers, however, are specifically exempted:

- Agricultural laborers.
- Persons employed in the domestic service of a family or person at his home.
- Individuals employed by spouse or parents.
- Independent contractors.
- Supervisory employees.
- Persons employed by employers subject to the Railway Labor Act.

The most important of these exceptions is that relating to supervisors. Prior to the 1947 Taft-Hartley amendments, supervisors were not excluded from the definition of "employee," and the employer could not discriminate against them for engaging in union activity. Since 1947, however, supervisors have not been protected by the Act. Supervisors still may join unions, if they so wish, but they may also be discharged for doing so, and there is nothing in the law that compels an employer to deal with any union they may designate to represent them. *(Parker-Robb Chevrolet, Food & Commercial Workers v. NLRB)*

If the effect of a supervisor's discharge is to intimidate nonsupervisory employees in the exercise of their rights under the Act, or if the supervisor's discharge serves as a "conduit" for the discharge of nonsupervisory union supporters, the NLRB may find a violation and order reinstatement. *(NLRB v. Better Monkey Grip Co., Sperry v. Brewery Workers Local 366, NLRB v. Downslope Industries, Inc.)* The discharge of a supervisor whose son was the chief union steward was unlawful, since the purpose of the discharge could only be to intimidate union supporters who were protected by the Act. *(NLRB v. Advertisers Manufacturing Co.)*

Included in the category of supervisors are those who have authority to hire and discharge, to adjust grievances, to make effective recommendations in such matters, or responsibly to direct their subordinates. The last attribute—responsibly to direct other employees—is sufficient to classify an employee as a "supervisor," even if all other marks of supervisory status are lacking. *(Ohio Power Co. v. NLRB)*

Nothing in the Act specifically excludes "managerial" and "confidential" workers from the definition of "employee." But the Supreme Court has held that managerial employees, who formulate and execute management decisions, are not covered by the Act *(NLRB v. Textron, Inc.)*, and that confidential employees, who assist and act in a confidential capacity to persons exercising managerial functions in labor-relations matters, should be excluded from employee bargaining units. *(NLRB v. Hendricks County Rural Electric Membership Corp.)* The Board holds, however, that confidential employees, unlike managerial employees, may not be discharged for engaging in union activity. *(Peavey Co. v. NLRB, Bentley Hedges Travel Service)*

The Supreme Court also has ruled that retirees are not "employees" covered by the Act. *(Chemical Workers v. Pittsburgh Plate Glass Co.)*

WHO IS AN "EMPLOYER"

In addition to employers whose operations do not affect interstate commerce, the Act exempts from its jurisdiction the following groups of employers:

- The Federal Government or any wholly owned government corporation or any federal reserve bank.
- Any state or political division of a state.
- Employers subject to the Railway Labor Act.
- Labor organizations, except when acting as employers.

The liability of an employer for actions that may violate the Act extends to the acts of the employer's "agents." This means, for one thing, that an employer may be held responsible for what one of his supervisors does as long as the supervisor was acting in his line of duty. This will be so even though the supervisor may not have been authorized to perform the particular act. But an employer may escape liability for isolated or sporadic instances of antiunion conduct by his supervisors, at least where there has been no approval of the conduct by the employer. *(NLRB v. Hinde & Dauch Paper Co., NLRB v. Brooks Cameras)*

3

EMPLOYEES' ORGANIZING RIGHTS

The rights of employees to organize into labor organizations and to bargain collectively with their employers are two of the basic rights guaranteed under the Act. To insure the free exercise of these rights, the Act makes certain actions by employers and unions unfair labor practices. It thus establishes ground rules for the conduct of organizing activities.

These rules drastically restrict what an employer may do once an organizing drive is under way. He may not restrain, coerce, or interfere with employees in the exercise of their rights under the law; he may not discriminate against employees because of their union activities or membership or because of their refusal to engage in such activities or to join the union; he may not dominate or assist a labor organization; and he may not refuse to recognize and bargain with a union duly selected to represent his employees.

WHAT IS "INTERFERENCE"

The unfair labor practice of "interference" is a broad one, embracing the more specific unfair practices of discrimination, domination, and refusal to bargain, plus a variety of additional acts. The acts forbidden range all the way from restraining the solicitation of union members to granting a wage increase during an organizing drive.

Suppose a union begins distributing literature and soliciting members in a plant. What restrictions may the employer lawfully place on the distribution and solicitation? The NLRB and the courts have laid down some specific rules on this. The important considerations are these: who is doing the soliciting or distribution, employees or outside organizers; where it takes place, on or off company property; and when it takes place, within or outside working time.

In brief, these are the rules:

- A no-solicitation, no-distribution rule is not unlawful merely because it is adopted during an organizing campaign. *(Brigadier Industries)*

- An employer may ban outside (nonemployee) union organizers from distributing literature or soliciting on company property if (1) the union may reach employees by making reasonable efforts through other available channels and (2) the no-solicitation order does not discriminate against the union by allowing other solicitation or distribution. *(NLRB v. Babcock & Wilcox Co., Central Hardware Co. v. NLRB, Hudgens v. NLRB)*

- An employer that permits the workplace to be disrupted by nonunion solicitations must permit union solicitation that is "substantially equivalent" to the nonunion solicitation in terms of interference with production and discipline. *(Restaurant Corp. of America v. NLRB)*

- Where an employer's own employees are concerned, (1) a rule forbidding distribution of union literature by employees in working areas will be presumptively valid even though it applies both to working and nonworking time; (2) a rule forbidding distribution on nonworking time in nonworking areas will be presumptively invalid; (3) a rule forbidding union solicitation by employees during their nonworking time will be presumptively invalid even though limited to working areas; and (4) a rule forbidding union solicitation during working time in any plant area will be presumptively valid. *(Stoddard-Quirk Manufacturing Co.)* Rules banning solicitation during "working time" are presumptively valid; rules banning solicitation during "working hours" are presumptively invalid. *(Our Way, Inc.)*

- There are exceptions where there are special circumstances making stricter rules necessary to maintain production or discipline. An example of such special circumstances is a retail store, in which solicitation may be forbidden in selling areas even during the employees' nonworking time. *(Marshall Field & Co., Walton Manufacturing Co., Stoddard-Quirk Manufacturing Co.)*
- If, however, a retail store enforces a broad no-solicitation rule forbidding union solicitation on the selling floors during both the working and nonworking time of the employees, officials of the store may not make speeches to "captive" audiences of employees on company time and property before a representation election unless the union is given an equal opportunity to reply. This is the so-called captive-audience rule, first enunciated by the NLRB in the *Bonwit-Teller* case and then revived in the 1962 *May Department Stores* decision. Such captive-audience speeches are considered both an unfair labor practice and grounds for setting an election aside, although at least one U.S. court of appeals does not agree with this holding.
- Hospitals have been permitted to ban solicitation, even on nonworking time, in corridors and sitting rooms on floors where patients' rooms or operating or therapy rooms were located, but not in areas such as cafeterias and gift shops. *(Beth Israel Hospital v. NLRB, NLRB v. Baptist Hospital)*
- An employer may bar off-duty employees from his plant, where (1) the no-access rule applies to entering the premises for any purpose, (2) it applies solely to the interior of the plant and other working areas, and (3) it is clearly disseminated to all employees. A rule meeting these requirements is presumptively valid absent a showing that no adequate alternative means of communication is available; a rule denying access to outside nonworking areas is invalid in the absence of business reasons justifying the rule. *(GTE Lenkurt, Tri-County Medical Center, East*

Bay Newspapers, Inc., NLRB v. Pizza Crust Co. of Pennsylvania)

- An incumbent union may not waive the rights of employees to distribute literature to co-workers in nonworking areas during nonworking time or to engage in in-plant solicitation on nonworking time. There had been a division of opinion on this issue, but the Supreme Court adopted the view that such a waiver would freeze out organizational efforts on behalf of a rival union. *(NLRB v. Magnavox Co.)*

Many other types of employer conduct have been held unlawful interference under the Act. The following are a few examples:

Questioning of Employees

For many years, the NLRB held that an employer's questioning of employees about their union activities or those of fellow employees of itself amounted to unlawful interference. The Board modified this position twice—first in 1954 and again in 1967. Under the current policy, an employer's polling of employees as to their union views will be considered unlawful, in the absence of unusual circumstances, unless (1) the purpose of the poll is to determine the truth of a union's claim of majority status; (2) the employees are told that this is the purpose of the poll; (3) assurance against reprisal is given; (4) the employees are polled by secret ballot; and (5) the employer has not engaged in unfair labor practices or otherwise created a coercive atmosphere. The Board emphasized the importance that the polling be done by secret ballot as giving further assurance "that reprisals cannot be taken against employees because the views of each individual will not be known." *(Blue Flash Express, Strusknes Construction Co.)*

Inquiry into the union sentiments of an open, active union supporter is not necessarily unlawful where no threats or promises are made. Factors that the Board examines include (1) background, (2) nature of the information sought, (3) identity of the questioner, and (4) place and method of interrogation. *(Rossmore House)*

If an employee is called to an interview that he reasonably believes may result in discipline, he is entitled to have a union representative present. *(NLRB v. Weingarten, Inc.)* He also is entitled to a pre-interview consultation with the person who will assist him at the interview and to be informed of the nature of the matter being investigated. *(Pacific Telephone & Telegraph Co.)* But such representation is not required at meetings held solely to inform employees of disciplinary decisions already made. *(Baton Rouge Water Works)*

The NLRB now holds that the right of representation at interviews exists only when there is a recognized or certified union. *(E.I. du Pont)* The Board has had several changes of mind on this issue, and the appeals courts disagree on this point. *(Anchortank v. NLRB, E.I. du Pont v. NLRB, Slaughter v. NLRB)*

The right of representation at interviews may be waived by an incumbent union. *(Prudential Insurance Co., Prudential Insurance Co. v. NLRB)*

A make-whole remedy, providing reinstatement and/or back pay, is issued if an employee is suspended or discharged for invoking his right to be represented at an interview. The Board formerly held that make-whole remedies could be appropriate where an employee was discharged or suspended for conduct that had been the subject of an interview at which the employee was unlawfully deprived of representation. The Board's current view is that it may not issue make-whole remedies in such situations. *(Taracorp, Communications Workers Local 5008 v. NLRB)*

Antiunion Petitions

The Act permits an employer to express noncoercive opinions of unions, but it does not permit him to inject himself directly into the business of getting employees to withdraw from a union. Circulating an antiunion petition may result in the employer's being found guilty of interference. *(Red Rock Co.)*

Increases in Wages and Other Benefits

Unilateral increases in wages or other benefits during a union organizing campaign have been regarded as a prime form of unlawful interference even though granted permanently and unconditionally. The same is true of a promise by the employer to increase wages or other benefits at a "crucial" time during a union organizing drive. There is an exception, however, where all the employer does is put into effect a regularly scheduled increase or one that had been decided upon and announced before the organizing campaign began. In fact, a delay or denial of a regularly scheduled increase during an organizing campaign might itself be unlawful interference. (*Medo Photo Supply Corp. v. NLRB, Standard Coil Products, Inc., Coca-Cola Bottling Co. v. NLRB, Bonwit Teller, Inc. v. NLRB, NLRB v. Exchange Parts Co.*)

Removal of Privileges

The removal of privileges enjoyed by employees or threats to take privileges away will constitute illegal interference where the object is to discourage union organization. (*NLRB v. Swan Fastener Corp.*)

Espionage and Surveillance

Although the use of "labor spies" is now a rarity, there have been a number of cases in which employers have been found to have engaged in unlawful interference by surveillance of their employees' union activities. The general rule is that any real check or guard maintained by management over union meetings or other union activities constitutes illegal interference "whether frankly open or carefully concealed." (*NLRB v. Collins & Aikman Corp.*)

Threat or Prediction

The courts have distinguished between a threat of retaliation for joining a union and a mere "prediction" of what may happen if a union won an election. Such a "prediction" is lawful if it is "carefully phrased on the basis of objective fact" to convey the employer's belief "as to demonstrably probable consequences beyond his control"; otherwise, it is an unlawful threat. (*NLRB v. Gissel Packing Co.*)

Discharge and Discipline

Even where there is no antiunion motivation, discharge or discipline may be unlawful if prompted by "concerted" activity, such as an employee's reasonable and honest invocation of a right set forth in his collective bargaining contract. (*NLRB v. City Disposal Systems*) In the NLRB's view, an employee who acts alone and is not seeking to enforce a collective bargaining contract may nonetheless be engaged in concerted activity if he is acting on the authority of co-workers. (*Meyers Industries*) Several appeals courts have endorsed the Board's definition of concerted activities, although one has done so reluctantly. (*Prill v. NLRB, Ewing v. NLRB*)

UNLAWFUL DISCRIMINATION

It is an unfair labor practice under Section 8(a)(4) of the Act for an employer to discharge or otherwise discriminate against an employee because he has filed charges or given testimony under the Act. This section protects an employee who gives a sworn statement to an NLRB field examiner investigating unfair labor practice charges against an employer. (*NLRB v. Scrivener*) The NLRB holds that Section 8(a)(4) protects supervisors as well as rank-and-file employees. (*General Services, Inc.*), but some courts disagree. (*Hi-Craft Clothing Co. v. NLRB*)

It is an unfair labor practice under Section 8(a)(3) of the Act for an employer to encourage or discourage union membership by discrimination with regard to hire or tenure of employment.

In determining whether an employer's discriminatory action encouraged or discouraged union membership, the NLRB and the courts look at a number of factors—the motive of the employer, his knowledge or lack of knowledge of the union activity, and his attitude toward unionization. "Subjective evidence" that the employees actually were encouraged or discouraged in their attitudes toward the union is not required. Where a natural consequence of the discrimination is encouragement or discouragement of union membership, it is presumed that the employer intended such consequences. Moreover, some acts, such as a grant of superseniority to strikers' replacements or grant of accrued vacation to replacements but not strikers, are regarded as so inherently discriminatory as to be unlawful without regard to the employer's motive. *(Radio Officer's Union v. NLRB, NLRB v. Erie Resistor Corp., NLRB v. Great Dane Trailers, Inc.)* But the Board has held that discrimination on the basis of race is not inherently destructive of employee rights and therefore is not a per se violation of the Act. *(Jubilee Manufacturing Co.; see Packinghouse Workers v. NLRB)*

Difficult questions under Section 8(a)(3) may be presented when it is alleged that the closing or moving of a plant was for antiunion reasons. Rulings of the NLRB and the courts in such cases include the following:

- An employer has the absolute right to close his entire business for any reason he chooses, including antiunion bias. *(Textile Workers v. Darlington Manufacturing Co., Darlington Manufacturing Co.)*

- An employer does not have a right to close part of his business, to transfer work to another plant, or to open a new plant to replace a closed plant, if the partial closing is motivated by a purpose to "chill" unionism in the remaining parts of the business and the employer reasonably can foresee that it will have that effect. *(Textile Workers v. Darlington Manufacturing Co., Darlington Manufacturing Co.)*

- Even if a partial closing is based on antiunion considerations—such as religious convictions against dealing with a union—this does not necessarily establish that a purpose of the closing was to "chill" unionism in the remainder of the business. *(A. C. Rochat Co.)*

- Transferring work for antiunion reasons is not unlawful if legitimate economic reasons would have led to the transfer in any event. *(Litton Systems)*

Section 8(a)(3) cases frequently involve allegations that an employer singled out union supporters for discharge or discipline. But this section places no obligations on the employer to avoid unfair or arbitrary treatment; as one court put it, an employee may be discharged "for a good reason, a poor reason, or no reason at all, so long as the terms of the statute are not violated." *(NLRB v. Condenser Corp. of America)*

Where a discharge or other discipline involves both union activity and a legitimate business reason, the NLRB applies a two-part causation test under which (1) the Board's General Counsel must make a prima facie showing that protected conduct was a motivating factor, and (2) the employer then has the burden of demonstrating that the same action would have occurred even in the absence of protected conduct. *(Wright Line, Inc., NLRB v. Transportation Management Corp.)*

In specific cases, the NLRB and the courts have considered such factors as the following in determining whether an employer's motive in discharging or otherwise disciplining employees was to encourage or discourage union membership:

Knowledge of Union Activity

To establish that an employee was discriminatorily discharged because of his union activities, it must be shown that the employer had knowledge of those activities. But in such cases, a supervisor's knowledge of the employee's activities will be imputed to the employer. *(McComb Manufacturing Co.)*

In some cases, the Board has held that a plant is so small that management may be assumed to know about the union activities of the employees in general and also those of various individual employees. *(National Paper Co.)* But one appeals court has said that this sort of inference did not constitute the substantial evidence required to establish employer knowledge. *(NLRB v. National Paper Co.)* Another court said that the small plant doctrine permits an inference of employer knowledge only if the Board establishes by other evidence that the employer had reason to notice the union activities. *(NLRB v. Health Care Logistics)*

Antiunion Background

If considerations appear more or less evenly balanced, the Board and the courts often will look for guidance to the employer's background attitude toward unions or employee organization. But the Board and the courts also may consider the lack of evidence of a "legitimate and substantial business justification" for the employer's action. *(Wyman-Gordon Co. v. NLRB, Valencia Service Co., NLRB v. Great Dane Trailers, Inc.)*

Unequal Enforcement of Plant Rules

If an employer discharges a union adherent for violating a rule that has not been enforced with respect to other employees, the Board may consider this evidence that the discharge was discriminatorily motivated. This would not be so if the employer could show that the rule had been applied uniformly to all employees. *(Stewart-Warner Corp., Shell Oil Co. v. NLRB)*

Timing of Discharge

The Board always looks with suspicion on the discharge or layoff of an employee immediately after the employer has learned of the employee's participation in union activity. In such a case, the Board will scrutinize closely the reason alleged by the employer as causing the discharge. *(NLRB v. Somerville Buick, Inc.)*

Questioning and Surveillance

If an employer has questioned an employee about his union membership or has asked someone to watch and see whether he attends union meetings, the employer already will have two strikes against him if he discharges the employee and charges of discrimination are filed. *(NLRB v. Swan Fastener Corp.)*

REINSTATEMENT AND BACK PAY

Where the NLRB has found that an employee was discharged unlawfully, it ordinarily will order that he be reinstated on unconditional application, even it this means discharging an employee who may have been hired to take his place. In a large proportion of the cases, the Board also will order the employer to make good to the employee any loss of wages he has suffered as a result of the discharge. If a union caused the employer to discharge the employee unlawfully, the back-pay order may be directed against either the union or the employer, or it may be directed against both.

In computing how much back pay is due a discriminatorily discharged employee, the NLRB gives weight to a number of factors—whether the employee has been offered reinstatement and when, whether the business of the employer was such that the employee may not have been employed during the entire period, whether the employee sought other work, whether he had earnings from another job. Here are some of the rules applied:

Terminating Liability

Although the back-pay bill may continue to mount until the employer complies with the order, the employer can terminate the increase at any time by an offer of reinstatement to the employee. If the employees accepts, he begins to draw wages again. If he unequivocally refuses reinstatement, the employer no longer is assessed with additions to the amount to be paid. *(Ford Motor Co.)*

Duty to Seek Work

An employee claiming back pay must have made a reasonable effort to obtain other work. If he fails to do so, the Board will deduct from the back pay the amount of wage losses willfully incurred. Registration with a government employment office will not be regarded as "conclusive proof" of a reasonable search for other work, but will be given greater or lesser weight depending on all the circumstances of the case. Diligence in making independent applications for jobs and use of other hiring facilities also will be considered. An employee generally need not accept another job to protect his back pay if it is not "substantially equivalent" to his former position (*Harvest Queen Mill & Elevator Co.*), but some courts have said that after looking for equivalent employment for a "reasonable" period of time, the employee should start looking for suitable jobs that are not necessarily equivalent to his former position. (*NLRB v. Southern Silk Mills, NLRB v. Madison Courier, Inc.*)

Discharged employees who conceal earnings from interim jobs are denied back pay for all calendar quarters in which they engage in the employment they have concealed. If their deception makes it impossible to attribute their interim employment to a specific quarter or quarters, they receive no back pay at all. (*American Navigation Co.*)

Offsets Against Back Pay

Where a discriminatorily discharged employee has obtained another job, the amount he earns in that job ordinarily will be deducted from the amount paid to him as back wages. If, however, the employee is put to extra expense to obtain or retain another job—for example, employment agency fees, commuting expenses above those usually incurred, or expenses required by living away from home—the extra expenses will not be deducted in computing "net earnings" at the interim job. (*Harvest Queen Mill & Elevator Co.*)

What Back Pay Includes

Basically, the back pay awarded to a discriminatorily discharged employee is intended to make him whole for earnings lost as a result of the discharge. As computed by the NLRB, the back pay will include: wage increases that would have been received but for the discharge computed from the date of discharge to the date of an offer of reinstatement (*A. P. W. Products Co.*); the increased pay from a promotion that would have been received but for the discharge (*Underwood Machinery Co.*); overtime pay that would have been earned but for the discharge *(Stover Bedding Co.)*; bonuses *(Dinion Coil Co.)*; and interest computed at the "short-term Federal rate" used by the U.S. Internal Revenue Service in calculating interest on the under-payment or overpayment of taxes. *(Isis Plumbing & Heating Co., Florida Steel Corp., New Horizons For The Retarded, Inc.)*

But the back pay will not cover periods when the employee would not have worked even if no discrimination had taken place. These include, for example, a period when the employee would have been laid off for economic reasons if he had not been laid off first for discriminatory reasons. *(NLRB v. Carolina Mills, Inc.)* They also include a period of sickness not covered by any sick leave policy of the employer. *(Harvest Queen Mill & Elevator Co.)*

ASSISTING OR DOMINATING UNION

In making it an unfair labor practice for an employer to dominate or assist a union, the Labor Relations Act was aiming at the so-called "company union"—a term often used in a derisive sense to indicate a company-dominated union. The NLRB, in its first two decisions under this ban as revised in 1947, held that there are two degrees of violation.

First, there are those cases involving employer's unfair practices that are so extensive as to constitute a domination of the labor organization. In such cases, the NLRB will order disestablishment of the organization, regardless of whether or not it is affiliated with the AFL-CIO. *(Carpenter Steel Co.)*

Second, there are those cases in which the unfair practices are limited to support and interference that never reached the point of domination. In these cases, the NLRB will "only order that recognition be withheld until certification, again without regard to whether or not the organization happens to be af-filiated." *(Hershey Metal Products Co.)*

Since whether a union has been dominated or assisted by an employer is a question of degree, no one fact ordinarily is conclusive. The U.S. Supreme Court has said that the "whole congeries of facts" presented to the NLRB may be considered in support of its findings. *(NLRB v. Link-Belt Co.)*

Unlawful support to a union may be either financial or nonfinancial. Where it is financial, the illegality is measured not in terms of its costs to the employer but in terms of its effect upon the recipient organization and the employees. *(Pacific Manifolding Book Co.)*

Some examples of unlawful *financial* support to a union are:

- Payment of employee representatives for time spent in committee meetings. *(NLRB v. General Shoe Corp.)*
- Loans to defray union expenses. *(Coal Creek Coal Co.)*
- Paying employees' union dues and initiation fees. *(NLRB v. Jack Smith Beverages, Inc.)*
- Permitting the union's operation of vending machines or concessions. *(Beaver Machine & Tool Co.)*

Some examples of unlawful *nonfinancial* support to a union are:

- Permitting use of company time and property for organizational or other union activities. *(NLRB v. Bradford Dyeing Association)*
- Recognition of, or execution of a contract with, the union without requiring proof of its majority status. There is, however, a special provision that permits an employer "primarily in the building and construction industry" to execute a contract with a union before it has established its majority status. *(NLRB v. Clark Phonograph Record Co.)*
- Falsely crediting the union with obtaining increases or other employee benefits. *(NLRB v. Clark Phonograph Record Co.)*
- Permitting a union to solicit dues-checkoff authorizations from new employees who are going through the hiring process. *(Alaska Salmon Industries)*

REMEDIES FOR "FLAGRANT" VIOLATIONS

Where the NLRB has found what it terms "flagrant" or "massive" violations, it has ordered remedies that go beyond the usual cease-and-desist order, reinstatement, and back pay.

Employers found guilty of such violations have been ordered to take the following actions:

- Convene work time meetings of employees and have a Board-dictated notice read to them. *(J. P. Stevens & Co. v. NLRB, Teamsters Local 115 v. NLRB)*
- Include copies of the Board's notice in appropriate company publications and publish it in newspapers of general circulation. *(Florida Steel Corp. v. NLRB, Teamsters Local 115 v. NLRB)*
- Give a union reasonable access to plant bulletin boards for a designated period of time. *(NLRB v. Elson Bottling Co., Teamsters Local 115 v. NLRB)*
- Replace general purpose bulletin boards, expressly permitting the posting of dissident union material or any other union material. *(Roadway Express v. NLRB)*
- Give a union reasonable access to employees in nonworking areas during nonworking time and permit the union to respond to any employer speech on the question of union representation. *(J. P. Stevens & Co. v. NLRB, Teamsters Local 115 v. NLRB; see Steelworkers v. NLRB)*
- Reimburse a union and the NLRB for their expenses in investigating, preparing, presenting, and conducting the case. *(J. P. Stevens & Co. v. NLRB)*
- Reimburse a union for all reasonable and necessary expenses incurred during an organizing campaign. *(J. P. Stevens & Co. v. NLRB)*

Even where the unfair labor practices are not "massive" or "flagrant," an employer may be ordered to pay litigation expenses, organizing costs, and attorneys' fees if it raises "frivolous" defenses. *(Heck's Inc., Autoprod, Inc.)*

Visitatorial Clause

The Board has denied a request by its General Counsel that a model visitatorial clause be routinely included in remedial orders. This type of clause would allow the Board to examine the books and records of a respondent and to take statements from its officers and employees for the purpose of determining or securing compliance with court-enforced orders. *(Cherokee Equity Corp.)* In one case, while refusing to issue a broad visitatorial clause, the Board included a limited visitatorial clause that required an employer to preserve and provide information relevant to the employer's claim that it had ceased operations and that another company was operating its facility. *(229 Lincoln Street, Inc.)*

4

Choosing A Bargaining Agent

A basic objective of the Labor Relations Act is to protect the right of employees to bargain collectively with their employer through a representative of their own choosing. This does not mean that each little group of organized employees may name its spokesman. Instead, the Act provides that all employees in an appropriate unit, whether members of the union or not, are to be represented by the organization that is chosen by the majority. And the Act establishes election machinery for choosing a majority representative.

Prior to the 1959 amendments to the Taft-Hartley Act, the NLRB itself decided whether and when an election should be held, what employees should be permitted to vote, and whether an election had been conducted under such circumstances as to ensure a free choice by the employees. The amendments, however, gave the Board power to delegate decision-making authority in election cases to its regional directors.

Exercising this authority, the Board gave its regional directors the power to handle the ordinary representation election and post-election challenges and objections. The regional directors also may rule on employer election petitions, decertification petitions, and requests for elections to rescind a union's authority to negotiate union-security contracts.

The Board, however, retained authority to rule on election issues where there is a stipulation for certification upon a consent election and on objections and challenges arising from

39

elections to rescind a union's authority to make union-security contracts. In all other cases, the regional director's decision on preelection and postelection issues is final unless review is granted by the Board.

WHO MAY ASK FOR ELECTION

A petition for a representation election may be filed by an employee, a group of employees, a union, or an employer. These are the rules:

Union Petitions

A union may petition for an election where either (1) it is seeking recognition as exclusive bargaining agent and the employer refuses to recognize it, or (2) it has been recognized but wants an election to obtain the benefits of a certification. (*Advance Pattern Co., General Box Co.*)

Except where an "expedited" election is sought under the provisions relating to recognition or organizational picketing, discussed below, the petition should be accompanied by proof that at least 30 percent of the employees in the unit are interested in having the union represent them.

Individual Petitions

An election petition filed by an individual, like one filed by a union, must be backed by a 30-percent showing of interest among the employees. Other than this, the individual need show only that he is seeking representative status for the purpose of collective bargaining. A petition may not, however, be filed by a supervisor. Since a supervisor may not represent employees for bargaining purposes, the NLRB will dismiss petitions filed by supervisors. (*Kennecott Copper Corp.*)

Employer Petitions

Except where the union is engaging in organizational or recognition picketing, an employer may petition for a representation election only if he is confronted with a demand by the union for exclusive bargaining recognition.

A formal request for recognition is not required, however. The Board will direct an election even if it is claimed that the employer has no reasonable basis for questioning the union's majority. *(J. C. Penney Co.)*

Other unions may be permitted to intervene in an election if they can show some interest in it—an existing contract with the employer, for example. They need not make a 30-percent showing of interest, however.

PETITIONS IN PICKETING CASES

A new Section 8(b)(7)(C) inserted in the Taft-Hartley Act by the Landrum-Griffin amendments makes it unlawful for a union to picket for recognition or organizational purposes if no election petition is filed within a reasonable period of time (not to exceed 30 days).

But when a petition is filed in one of these cases, the NLRB must direct an election "forthwith" without regard to the usual requirements that (1) an employer petition be based on a demand for recognition by the union, (2) a union petition be based on a 30-percent showing of interest among the employees, and (3) the Board first conduct an investigation and hearing.

This section of the law is discussed in more detail in Chapter 7.

DETERMINING BARGAINING UNIT

Subject to certain limitations, the Labor Management Relations Act confers on the NLRB the authority to determine in each case what the appropriate bargaining unit shall be. This could be, for example, an employerwide unit, a plant unit, a craft unit, or a departmental unit.

The 1947 Taft-Hartley amendments, however, placed some express limitations on the NLRB's authority in the determination of bargaining units. These include:

- The extent to which employees have organized a union shall not be controlling. If, for example, a union has organized one department of a plant or a part of a department, the NLRB may not direct an election among those particular employees just because the union has not been able to organize employees elsewhere in the plant. Extent of organization, however, may be one of several factors considered by the Board to justify a certain unit. *(NLRB v. Metropolitan Life Insurance Co.)*
- Professional employees may not be included in a unit with nonprofessionals unless a majority of the professional employees vote for this inclusion in a separate self-determination election.
- Guards may not be included in the same bargaining unit with nonguards. The only appropriate unit covering guards is one that is limited exclusively to guards. Furthermore, a guard union may not be certified if it takes persons other than guards into membership or is affiliated, directly or indirectly, with a union that represents persons other than guards.
- In ruling on requests for a unit of skilled craftsmen and their helpers and apprentices to be severed from a broader unit, the Board is limited by a craft unit proviso to Section 9 of the Act. (Craft severance elections are discussed in more detail below.)

PERSONS EXCLUDED FROM UNIT

In addition to these limitations on the Board's authority to determine appropriate bargaining units, the Act requires that certain types of employees be excluded from the unit regardless of the type of unit. The principal class of exclusions consists of persons identified with management's interest. Excluded are supervisors, independent contractors, agricultural laborers, domestics, anyone employed by his parent or spouse, and those covered by the Railway Labor Act.

The Supreme Court has held that "managerial" employees—defined by the NLRB as those who formulate and effectuate management policies by expressing and making operative the decisions of their employer—are not covered by the Act. *(NLRB v. Textron Inc.)* This exclusion applied to university faculty members who were managerial employees, the Court later held, even though they came within the Act's definition of "professional employees." *(NLRB v. Yeshiva University)*

The Court has upheld the Board's practice of excluding employees who are closely related to members of management, even though these employees do not enjoy special job-related privileges. *(NLRB v. Action Automotive)*

The Board also excludes confidential employees who assist and act in a confidential capacity to persons exercising managerial functions in labor-relations matters *(NLRB v. Hendricks County Rural Electric Membership Corp.)*, children and spouses of persons holding substantial stock interests in closely held corporations *(Foam Rubber City #2 of Florida, Inc.)*, management "trainees" *(Curtis Noll Corp.)*, and temporary employees, including students hired during school vacations. *(Westinghouse Air Brake Co.)*

But probationary and regular part-time employees are not excluded *(National Torch Tip Co., Booth Broadcasting Co.)*, nor are employees on vacation or other authorized leave of absence. Employees will not be excluded merely because they are limiting their working time and earnings to avoid decreasing their social security annuities. *(NLRB v. Holiday Inn of Oak Ridge, Tenn.)*, but retired employees who are no longer working for the employer at all are not "employees" within the meaning of the Act. *(Chemical Workers v. Pittsburgh Plate Glass Co.)* Laid-off employees and those absent because of illness will be included if they have a reasonable expectation of returning to work. *(Sportswear Industries, Inc., Sullivan Surplus Sales, Inc.)*

Working within the statutory limitations, the NLRB has developed some tests of its own for determining appropriate bargaining units. One basic principle it has laid down is that the unit determined need not be the *only* appropriate unit, or the *ultimate* unit, or the *most* appropriate unit. It is necessary only that the unit be "appropriate." Thus, the Board sometimes finds that alternate units are appropriate and lets the employees determine which unit they approve in so-called self-determination elections.

Among the principal factors the Board considers in determining whether particular units are appropriate are the following:

- The similarity of duties, skills, wages, and working conditions of the employees involved.
- The pertinent collective bargaining history, if any, among the employees involved. Also, in some instances, the history, extent, and type of union organization in other plants of the same company or the same industry.
- The extent and type of union organization of the employees involved, although the Board is forbidden by the statute to make the extent of organization the controlling factor.
- The employees' own wishes in the matter. This refers only to those cases involving professional employees, employees with certain craft skills, and certain other groups where the Board permits employees to vote separately on the question of whether they should be placed in a unit limited to their own group or placed in a larger unit. These are called self-determination elections.
- The appropriateness of the units proposed in relation to the organizational structure of the company itself.

CRAFT, DEPARTMENTAL UNITS

Under Section 9(b) of the Act, the NLRB is forbidden to "decide that any craft unit is inappropriate . . . on the ground that a different unit has been established by a prior Board determination, unless a majority of the employees in the proposed craft unit vote against separate representation."

National Tube Decision

In its 1948 *National Tube* decision, the Board appeared to give this proviso only limited significance. It construed the proviso as not barring it from considering prior determinations and bargaining history as long as neither was made the sole ground for the decision.

On this basis, the Board decided that craft severance elections should not be directed in the basic steel industry in view of the integrated nature of operations in the industry and the history of bargaining on an industrial, rather than craft, basis. This policy of denying craft severance elections later was extended to three other "integrated" industries—wet milling, lumber, and aluminum. (*Corn Products Refining Co., Weyerhaeuser Timber Co., Permanente Metals Corp.*)

American Potash Decision

In the 1954 *American Potash* case, the Board took a new look at the craft severance problem and changed its policy. It decided that henceforth craft units must be split off from an established industrial unit whenever (1) the unit sought to be severed is a "true craft group," and (2) the union seeking severance traditionally has represented employees in the craft. But the Board did rule that it would not permit craft severance in the four industries covered by the *National Tube* doctrine.

Mallinckrodt Chemical Decision

In 1966, the Board decided to revise its rules on craft severance elections completely. Henceforth, the Board said, it will consider all areas relevant to an informed decision in craft severance cases, including the following: (1) whether the proposed unit embraces a distinct and homogeneous group of skilled craftsmen performing the functions of their craft on a nonrepetitive basis; (2) the bargaining history of employees and the plant and other plants of the employer; (3) the extent to which the employees have maintained their separate identity during their inclusion in the broader unit; (4) the history and pattern of bargaining in the industry; (5) the degree of integration of the employer's production processes; (6) the qualifications of the union seeking to represent a severed unit. Both the *American Potash* and the *National Tube* decisions were revised in accordance with these principles.

MULTIPLANT OPERATIONS

When a union seeks a unit confined to one plant of an employer engaged in a multiplant operation, the NLRB uses the following principles:

- A single-plant unit is presumptively appropriate for bargaining.

- Unless the single-plant unit sought has been so effectively merged into a more comprehensive unit by bargaining history, or is so integrated with another plant as to destroy its separate identity, it is an appropriate bargaining unit even though another unit, if requested, also might be appropriate.

- Unless an appropriate unit compatible with that requested by the union does not exist, the union need not seek representation in any larger unit or in the most comprehensive unit. (*Dixie Belle Mills, Inc.*)

Retail Chains, Insurance Companies

At one time, the NLRB treated retail chain operations and insurance companies differently from other businesses. It held that retail units should embrace all stores in an employer's administrative division or geographic area, and that only statewide or employerwide units of insurance agents were appropriate. The Board has abandoned this policy, however, and now applies the same basic rules to multifacility operations in general. (*Quaker City Life Insurance Co., Sav-On Drugs, Inc.*)

The Board's bargaining unit policy with regard to retail chain operations is set out at length in the *Haag Drug* decision.

INDUSTRY UNITS

Among the bargaining unit findings that have been made in various industries are the following:

Banks

The same basic principles apply to multifacility banking establishments as to other chain operations, and a single-bank unit therefore is presumed appropriate. *(Wyandotte Savings Bank, Alaska State Bank; but see Wayne Oakland Bank v. NLRB)*

Department Stores

An overall unit of selling and nonselling employees is the optimum unit, but separate units of sales, nonsales, clerical, and restaurant employees also have been found appropriate. *(Stern's, Paramus Retail Store Union v. NLRB)*

Grocery Stores

An overall unit is appropriate. Separate units of meat department employees and of employees who handle groceries and produce also have been found appropriate. *(Weis Markets, Inc.)*

Health Care Institutions

The appropriateness of requested health care units is determined through use of a "disparity of interests" test under which "normal" unit criteria are applied but "sharper than usual differences" between wages, hours, and working conditions of employees in the proposed unit and those in an overall professional or nonprofessional unit must be demonstrated in order for a separate unit to be approved. *(St. Francis Hospital)*

One appeals court found that this disparity of interests test was based on the Board's misinterpretation of the statute *(Electrical Workers (IBEW) Local 474 v. NLRB)*, but the Board adhered to this standard, stating that it had modified, not radically departed from, its approach under which traditional "community of interests" criteria were applied whenever a requested unit fell within one of seven basic employee groupings that the Board regarded as potentially appropriate health care units. *(St. Francis Hospital)*

Other courts have approved both the disparity of interests test and the community of interests test. *(Southwest Community Health Svcs. v. NLRB, NLRB v. HMO International, Trustees of Masonic Hall v. NLRB, Watonwan Memorial Hospital v. NLRB)*

The Board, in the exercise of its rulemaking authority, has issued a notice of proposed rulemaking that would establish eight appropriate bargaining units in the health-care industry. The Board continues to apply its disparity-of-interests test pending issuance of the rule. *(St. Vincent Hospital)*

Bargaining history is a factor that the Board considers in determining health care units, but it is not controlling. *(St. Luke's Memorial Hospital)*

A unit of hospital housestaff—interns, residents, and fellows—is not appropriate for bargaining, in the NLRB's view, since it is "primarily students" rather than employees. *(Physicians National House Staff Association v. Fanning, Physicians National House Staff Association v. Murphy)* But health-care employees and non-health-care employees may be included in a single bargaining unit. *(Oklahoma Blood Institute)*

Hotels and Motels

A unit of all of a hotel's employees has been found appropriate, but the Board will approve a less than overall unit, such as a unit of engineering employees, if the functions and interests of all employees are not so highly integrated as to require an overall unit. *(Wayside Realty Group, Inc., Omni-Dunfey Hotels)*

Utilities

The systemwide unit is the optimum one for utilities, such as power, telephone, and gas companies. Systemwide units have been found appropriate despite a history of bargaining for smaller units. But single-plant units also may be appropriate in some circumstances. *(Duquesne Light Co., Ohio Bell Telephone Co., Philadelphia Electric Co., Pacific Gas & Electric Co.)*

Pipeline operations are more highly integrated than most utilities, the Board has said, and therefore it is reluctant to fragmentize them, absent compelling circumstances. *(Michigan Wisconsin Pipe Line Co.)*

NAMES AND ADDRESSES RULE

As part of its direction of election, the NLRB may require the employer to provide a list of the names and addresses of all employees eligible to vote in the election. *(Excelsior Underwear, Inc.)* The Board then gives the list to the union or any other party to the election.

The Board's authority to require an employer to provide such a list was upheld by the Supreme Court in the *Wyman-Gordon* case. The Court said that the Board's direction to supply the list of names and addresses was an order the company was obligated to obey.

CONDUCTING THE ELECTION

If the unit sought in the petition is not appropriate, the NLRB regional director will not go ahead with the election. He also will not hold an election on the petition of one union if the employer has a current and valid contract with another union. This contract-bar doctrine and its exceptions are discussed later in this chapter.

Assuming there are no bargaining unit or contract-bar issues, the regional director will set the machinery for holding the election into motion. If the parties are in agreement, the election will be a consent election and informal procedures will be used. If there is no agreement, the election will be directed after a hearing.

The particular day selected for the election usually will be one when substantially all eligible employees will have a chance to vote. The voting hours will be arranged so that all eligible voters on all shifts will have adequate opportunity to vote.

The location of the polling places is determined with a view to easy accessibility to the voters. The Board's regional director usually tries to have the election conducted on company property. He has discretion to determine whether mail ballots should be used. If mail ballots are used, an individual should not be permitted to pick up a ballot for another potential voter in the election. *(Brink's Armored Car)*

Official notices of the election are posted in the plant several days before the election. An employer's failure to post the notices may be reason to set the election aside. *(Teamsters Local 148)* However, an employer may not invalidate an election by refusing to post notices. Board agents will undertake to publicize the election under such circumstances. *(Falmouth Co.)*

The notice of election usually contains a sample copy of the ballot. Defacement or marking of the posted sample ballots is no reason for the Board to set aside the election, unless one of the parties is responsible for the defacement. *(Murray Chair Co.)*

PREELECTION PROPAGANDA

The Board repeatedly has said that it generally will not censor or police the preelection propaganda of the parties. But there are limitations on such campaign techniques as (1) reproduction of the official ballot, (2) forged documents, (3) speech-making immediately before the election, and (4) racial, religious, or ethnic slurs. Here are some of the rules:

- Distribution of sample NLRB ballots marked "no union" or for one of the competing unions invalidates an election if the altered ballot gave voters the misleading impression that the Board favored one of the parties. No such impression is created when the party responsible for the reproduction is clearly identified on its face, but when the source of the altered ballot is not so identified, the Board examines the nature and contents of the material distributed to determine whether it had a tendency to mislead. *(Allied Electric Products, SDC Investment)*

- The Board will not permit the use of forged documents that leave the voters unable to recognize propaganda for what it is. *(United Aircraft Corp., Midland National Life Insurance Co.)* But the Board no longer probes into the truth or falsity of campaign statements or sets elections aside on the basis of misleading campaign statements.

(Midland National Life Insurance Co., Riveredge Hospital, W. R. Grace & Co.)

- Employers and unions are prohibited from making election speeches to massed assemblies of employees on company time within 24 hours before the election. *(Peerless Plywood Co.)*
- A retail store that forbids union solicitation in selling areas during both the employees' working and nonworking time must give the union equal opportunity to reply to any speech by an official of the store on company time and property. *(May Department Stores Co.)*
- Irrelevant and inflammatory racial appeals that are neither truthful nor germane to the election issues will be grounds for setting an election aside. *(Sewell Manufacturing Co., Allen-Morrison Sign Co.)* The same rule has been applied to religious and ethnic slurs. *(NLRB v. Silverman's Men's Wear, Inc., NLRB v. Katz)* But a single statement involving a racial epithet that was made in the first of seven union meetings more than one month before the election did not warrant setting the election aside. *(Beatrice Grocery)* And a rerun election properly was scheduled 67 days after a union official's religious slur that was the basis for overturning the first election. *(NLRB v. Carl Weissman & Sons)*
- Electioneering in and around the polls is grounds for setting the election aside. In most cases, the Board will fix a "no-electioneering" area which usually will be a circle with a radius of 100 feet around the polling place. *(Mutual Distributing Co.)*
- Conversations the parties have with employees who are in the polling area waiting to vote will usually invalidate the election. The Board will not inquire into the content of the conversation. *(Milchem, Inc.)*
- Keeping a list of employees who have voted—other than the official eligibility list used to check off voters as they receive their ballots—invalidates the election. *(Sound Refining, Cerock Wire & Cable)*
- Threats of retaliation against employees if they vote for the union or promises of benefits if they vote against it

are grounds for setting aside an election. These also may be unfair labor practices. But statements that are not sufficiently coercive to constitute an unfair labor practice still may be the basis for setting an election aside when considered in the light of the "economic realities" of the employer-employee relationship. *(Lord Baltimore Press)*

- Union threats of post-election picket-line violence may interfere with an election even if the threats do not relate to how the employees vote. *(Industrial Disposal Service)*
- A union may not make a preelection offer to waive initiation fees if the offer is extended only to those who sign authorization cards before the election. *(NLRB v. Savair Manufacturing Co.)* Such an offer not only invalidates the election but constitutes an unfair labor practice. *(Teamsters Local 420 (Gregg Industries))* But unions may offer to waive or reduce initiation fees for all employees, whether they join before or after the election. *(B. F. Goodrich Tire Co.)*

COUNTING THE BALLOTS

Each party to an election may appoint observers to act as checkers at the polls, assist in the counting of ballots, assist in the identification of voters, challenge voters, and otherwise assist the Board agent. Unless the parties agree otherwise, the observers must be nonsupervisory employees.

The counting of the ballots, however, may be observed by other persons designated by the parties, including supervisors and executives. Unless there is agreement among all the observers, the Board agent makes the determination as to the validity of a ballot. Any party may press its disagreement with the determination by filing timely objections.

CERTIFICATION OF UNION

If no objections to the election are filed or if those that are filed are rejected, the Board then will issue a certification. There are two main types of certification: (1) a certification of representative, which is issued after an election in which a majority of the employees voted for a union; and (2) a certificate of the results of the election, which is issued after an election in which a majority of the employees failed to vote for union representation.

There are a number of benefits that accrue to the union—and some to the employer—from a certification. For example:

- The employer must bargain with the certified union for at least one year. *(Brooks v. NLRB)*
- A certified union may strike to force the employer to assign work to members of the union in accordance with the certification. This is discussed in more detail in Chapter 7.
- A rival union may not engage in a strike or picketing for recognition in the face of the certification. This also is discussed in more detail in the later chapter.
- Even if the parties do not sign a collective bargaining contract, a rival union normally will not be able to petition for an election within a year of the certification.
- If a contract is signed within a year of certification, it usually will bar a rival union's petition for the contract's duration up to a maximum of three years under the so-called contract-bar rules.

CONTRACT-BAR RULES

One of the prime purposes of the Taft-Hartley Act is to promote stable employer-union relationships under contracts covering terms and conditions of employment. In pursuit of this objective, the NLRB has established the contract-bar doctrine. In brief, the doctrine is that a current and valid contract between an employer and a union ordinarily will bar an election sought by a rival union.

The doctrine is not mentioned in the Act itself or in any regulations of the Board. It has been laid down in a long line of decisions by the Board. These decisions have woven a complex pattern of rules—rules that establish when a contract will operate as an election bar and when a rival union's election petition will be recognized and processed. Here are some of the main points:

- A union-security contract that is "clearly unlawful on its face" or that has been found unlawful in an unfair labor practice proceeding will not bar an election. But a contract may bar an election even though it contains a hot-cargo clause that is unlawful under the Act. *(Food Haulers, Inc., Paragon Products Corp.)*

- Any contract of definite duration with a term of up to three years will bar an election for its entire term. A contract lasting longer than three years will bar an election sought by an outside union only for its first three years, but it will bar an election sought by the company or contracting union (if certified) for its full term. *(Montgomery Ward & Co., General Cable Corp.)*

- Contracts having no fixed duration are not considered an election bar for any period. *(Pacific Coast Association of Pulp & Paper Manufacturers)*

- A petition filed during the term of an existing contract will be considered timely and will be processed only if it is filed more than 60 days but not more than 90 days before the termination date of the contract. *(Leonard Wholesale Meats)*

- A contract that is prematurely extended will not bar an election if the petition is filed over 60 but not more than 90 days before the expiration date of the original contract. *(Deluxe Metal Furniture Co.)*

- Notice to modify or actual modification of a contract during its term will not remove the contract as a bar to an election. *(Deluxe Metal Furniture Co.)*

- A petition filed by a rival union during the 60-day period preceding the expiration of a contract will not be entertained by the Board even though the contract contains an automatic renewal clause. A petition filed after the expiration date of an automatic renewal contract will be accepted only if (1) the employer and the incumbent union have failed to execute a new contract during the 60-day period, (2) automatic renewal was forestalled by timely notice of one of the parties, and (3) the rival union's petition was filed prior to the execution of a new contract. *(Deluxe Metal Furniture Co.)*

- A schism within a union will remove a contract as a bar to an election where (1) there is a basic intraunion conflict; (2) this conflict has resulted in such action by the employees that stability can be restored only by an election; (3) there has been an open meeting, with due notice, for the purpose of considering disaffiliation; (4) a disaffiliation vote was taken within a reasonable period after the conflict arose; and (5) the employer is faced with conflicting representation claims. A "basic intraunion conflict" was found by the Board to exist both in the cases of the unions expelled from the CIO on charges of Communism and those expelled from the AFL-CIO on charges of corruption. *(Lawrence Leather Co., Great Atlantic & Pacific Tea Co., Hershey Chocolate Corp.)*

DECERTIFICATION ELECTIONS

A union may lose, as well as win, a certification as bargaining representative in the NLRB-conducted election. A petition for an election to decertify a union may be filed by a union, an employee, or a group of employees. But such a petition may not be filed by either an employer or a supervisor.

There is a 30-percent requirement for decertification, as well as representation, elections. The Board will direct a decertification election only if 30 percent of the employees in the unit support the petition. The contract-bar and other Board election rules apply to decertification elections in the same way that they apply to representation elections. But the only appropriate unit for a decertification election is the unit covered by the certification. The Board, for example, will not entertain a decertification petition by a group of craftsmen who are part of a plantwide production and maintenance unit. *(Campbell Soup Co.)*

CARD-CHECK BARGAINING ORDERS

The NLRB's authority to issue a bargaining order on the basis of authorization cards was upheld in the Supreme Court's *Gissel Packing* decision. The Court made the following points:

- Even in the absence of a demand for recognition or an unlawful refusal of recognition, a bargaining order may issue where this is the only available effective remedy for substantial unfair labor practices.

- The Board may issue a bargaining order in less extraordinary cases marked by less pervasive practices which nonetheless have a tendency to undermine majority strength and impede the election process. If a union has attained majority status and the possibility of erasing the effects of past practices and of ensuring a fair election through traditional remedies is "slight," a bargaining order may issue.

- There is a third category of minor or less extensive unfair labor practices having only minimal effect on the election machinery; these will not sustain a bargaining order.

Unless a union achieves majority status in an appropriate unit at some relevant time, the NLRB will not issue a bargaining order even if the employer whom the union is trying to organize commits outrageous and pervasive unfair labor practices. *(Gourmet Foods)* The federal appeals courts differ on whether such nonmajority bargaining orders ever are permissible. *(United Dairy Farmers Cooperative Association v. NLRB, Conair Corp. v. NLRB)*

The NLRB's view is that the propriety of issuing a bargaining order should be judged as of the time the employer's unfair labor practices were committed, not in light of later events. *(Gibson Products Co.)* Some appeals courts have disagreed, finding that changed circumstances such as employee turnover and new management must be considered. *(Clark's Gamble Corp. v. NLRB, General Steel Products, Inc. v. NLRB, NLRB v. Gibson Products Co., NLRB v. Windsor Industries, Impact Industries v. NLRB)*

An employer's obligation under a card-based bargaining order commences as of the time he embarks on a clear course of unlawful conduct or has engaged in sufficient unfair labor practices to undermine the union's majority. (*Steel-Fab, Inc., Trading Port, Inc., Beasley Energy, Inc.*)

Bernel Foam Doctrine

For 10 years prior to May 1964, a union that went to an NLRB election was precluded from filing an unfair labor practice charge based on the employer's refusal to recognize it prior to the election. But in May 1964, the Board announced the *Bernel Foam* doctrine, under which a union that proceeds to an election and loses it may file a postelection charge alleging that the employer unlawfully refused to recognize it before the election and that a bargaining order therefore should issue. No bargaining order will issue unless (1) there were objections to the election in the representation case and (2) the misconduct warrants voiding the election. (*Irving Air Chute Co. v. NLRB*)

A union that is refused recognition, despite authorization cards purporting to show majority status, has the burden of invoking the NLRB's election processes unless the employer has committed unfair labor practices. In the absence of an agreement to permit majority status to be determined by a means other than an NLRB election, an employer is not obligated to petition for an NLRB election in response to a union's card-based claim of majority status. (*Linden Lumber Div., Summer & Co. v. NLRB*) But where an employer takes his own poll to determine whether the union has a majority, he is bound by the results of the poll if it shows that the union does have majority status. (*Soil Mechanics Corp., Sullivan Electric Co. v. NLRB; see Snow & Sons v. NLRB*)

5

THE DUTY TO BARGAIN

The duty to bargain under the Taft-Hartley Act is two-edged. An employer is obligated to bargain in good faith with a union representing a majority of the employees in an appropriate unit. And a majority union is obligated to bargain in good faith with the employer. But neither is required "to agree to a proposal" made by the other or to make "a concession."

SUBJECTS FOR BARGAINING

The Act specifies that an employer and a majority union must bargain in good faith concerning wages, hours, and other terms and conditions of employment. Going on from there, the NLRB—with the approval of the U.S. Supreme Court—has recognized three categories of bargaining proposals and has established three sets of rules for them. They are:

- *Illegal Subjects.* These are the demands that would be illegal and forbidden under the Act, such as a proposal for a closed shop. Bargaining on these subjects may not be required, and they may not be included in the contract even if the other party agrees.
- *Voluntary Subjects.* These are the topics that fall outside the mandatory category of "wages, hours, and other conditions of employment." They may be placed on the bargaining table for voluntary bargaining and agreement. The other party, however, may not be required either to bargain on them or to agree to their inclusion in a con-

tract. Insistence on them as a condition to the execution of a contract will be a violation of the bargaining duty.

- *Mandatory Subjects.* These are the subjects that fall within the category of "wages, hours, and other terms and conditions of employment." Both the employer and the union are required to bargain in good faith with respect to them. *(NLRB v. Wooster Division, Borg-Warner Co.)*

MANDATORY BARGAINING SUBJECTS

The category of mandatory subjects of bargaining has been given specific meaning by a long line of NLRB and court decisions. Included in the category, for example, are such topics as:

- Discharge of employees. *(National Licorice Co. v. NLRB)*
- Seniority, grievances, and working schedules. *(Inland Steel Co. v. NLRB, United States Gypsum Co., NLRB v. Hallam & Boggs Truck Co.)*
- Union security and checkoff. *(NLRB v. Andrew Jergens Co., NLRB v. Reed & Prince Manufacturing Co.)*
- Vacations and individual merit raises. *(NLRB v. Allison & Co., Phelps Dodge Copper Products Corp.)*
- Retirement and pension and group insurance plans. *(Inland Steel Co. v. NLRB, Cross & Co. v. NLRB)*
- Christmas bonuses and profit-sharing retirement plan. *(NLRB v. Niles-Bement-Pond Co., NLRB v. Black-Clawson Co.)*
- Employee stock purchase plan providing for employer contributions and making benefits partly dependent on length of service. *(Richfield Oil Co. v. NLRB)*
- A nondiscriminatory union hiring hall. *(Associated General Contractors)*
- Plant rules on rest or lunch periods. *(National Grinding Wheel Co., Inc.)*
- Safety rules, even though the employer may be under legal obligation to provide safe and healthful conditions of employment. *(NLRB v. Gulf Power Co.)*

- Company-owned houses occupied by the employees, as well as the rent paid for the houses. *(NLRB v. Hart Cotton Mills, Inc., American Smelting & Refining Co. v. NLRB)*

- No-strike clauses binding on all employees in the bargaining unit. *(Shell Oil Co., Lloyd A. Fry Roofing Co.)*

- Physical examinations employees are required to take. *(Leroy Machine Co.)*

- Insurance plans, even though the employer proposed to improve the insurance programs and the expiring agreement contained no provisions concerning the plans. *(Borden, Inc.)*

- The privilege of exclusive hunting on a reserved portion of the company's forest preserve, a privilege that had existed for 20 years before the company proposed to discontinue it. *(Southland Paper Mills, Inc.)*

- A "bar list" maintained by an oil company of former employees and others who were barred from entering the company's refineries. *(Shell Oil Co.)*

- "Most favored nation" clauses. *(Dolly Madison Industries)*

- Polygraph (lie detector) tests for employees. *(Medicenter, Mid-South Hospital)*

- A "zipper clause" closing out bargaining during the term of the contract and making the contract the exclusive statement of the parties' rights and obligations. *(NLRB v. Tomco Communications, Inc.)*

- Jury-duty rights. *(NLRB v. Merrill & Ring)*

- The preparation, use, and sharing of costs of official transcripts of arbitration hearings. *(Communications Workers)*

- A plan under which employees could purchase the employer's products at a discount. *(Owen-Corning Fiberglas Corp.)*

- A recreation fund that subsidized activities suggested by employees, even though the fund was established unilaterally by the employer who had sole discretion over disbursements. *(Getty Refining & Marketing Co.)*

The Board has indicated, in an advice memorandum, that drug/alcohol testing of employees is a mandatory subject of bargaining. *(Reynolds Electrical and Engineering Co.)*

An employer whose in-plant food services are managed by an independent caterer must bargain over in-plant food services and prices, the Supreme Court has held. But the Court left open the question whether an employer who does not have in-plant food services must bargain over a union's demand that they be established. *(Ford Motor Co. v. NLRB)*

Plant Closing; Subcontracting

An employer has an absolute right to close his entire business for any reason he pleases. *(Textile Workers v. Darlington Manufacturing Co.)* An employer who closes all or part of his business for economic reasons need not bargain about the decision to close but must bargain about the effects of the decision on his employees. *(Merryweather Optical Co., First National Maintenance Corp. v. NLRB)*

An employer that decided to sell a dealership facility was required to bargain over the effects of this decision on employees, the NLRB held, but not over the decision itself. Decisions that involve "a significant investment or withdrawal of capital" and "affect the scope and ultimate direction of an enterprise" lie at "the very core of entrepreneurial control" and are not mandatory subjects of bargaining, the Board said. *(General Motors Corp., Auto Workers Local 864 v. NLRB)*

Bargaining was required over an economically motivated decision to subcontract bargaining-unit work to an outside firm, the U.S. Supreme Court held, emphasizing that the subcontract did not alter the employer's basic operation, but merely replaced existing employees with those of a contractor to do the same work under similar conditions. The Court limited its holding to "the facts of the case" and said its ruling did not encompass other forms of subcontracting. *(Fibreboard Paper Products Corp. v. NLRB)*

In the leading *Otis Elevator* case, the NLRB held that an employer's decision to discontinue research and development activities at a New Jersey facility and to consolidate these activities with operations at a Connecticut facility was not a mandatory subject of bargaining. There was no majority opinion, but all four Board members reached the same result on the mandatory-subject point and on the need for a uniform test applicable to all subcontracting, relocation, reorganization, and other economically motivated decisions to remove work from a union's bargaining unit. *(Otis Elevator Co.)*

At least one court has approved the Board's *Otis Elevator* standard. *(Steelworkers Local 2179 v. NLRB)* The court indicated that the *Otis Elevator* standard—under which an employer's major business conduct decision is not subject to mandatory bargaining unless the decision turns upon labor costs—is reasonable as applied to plant relocations. But another appeals court has disagreed with the Board's "turns on labor costs" distinction. The court found an employer was not required to bargain over an economically motivated decision to close one plant and transfer the work to another facility, even though the Board had found that the decision turned on labor costs. *(Arrow Automotive Industries v. NLRB)*

The Board, applying its *Otis Elevator* standard, ruled that an economically motivated decision to lay off employees is a mandatory subject of bargaining, but that compelling economic considerations may excuse an employer's failure to bargain over the layoff decision. *(Lapeer Foundry)*

The Board no longer requires an employer to obtain the consent of an incumbent union before transferring work from a facility covered by the union's labor agreement to a nonunion facility where labor costs will be lower. *(Milwaukee Spring Division of Illinois Coil Spring Co.)* The D.C. Circuit has gone beyond the Board in holding that because the right to relocate work was given by contract, the employer was not required even to bargain to impasse with the union. *(Auto Workers v. NLRB (Milwaukee Spring Division of Illinois Coil Spring Co.))* Other courts do require bargaining to impasse. *(University of Chicago v. NLRB, Boeing Co.)*

The Board will not order bargaining "where the decision is predicated on economic factors so compelling that bargaining could not alter them." *(Brooks-Scanlon, Inc., Lumber & Sawmill Workers Local 1017 v. NLRB)*

VOLUNTARY BARGAINING SUBJECTS

There has not been as much delineation of voluntary subjects of bargaining—those that may be advanced but not insisted
upon as a condition to an agreement. The following, however,
have been placed in this category: (1) a clause making the local
union the exclusive bargaining agent, even though the international union was the certified agent *(NLRB v. Wooster Division,
Borg-Warner)*; (2) a clause requiring a secret ballot vote among
the employees on the employer's last offer before a strike could
be called *(NLRB v. Wooster Division, Borg-Warner)*; (3) a clause
fixing the size and membership of the union grievance committee *(Iron Castings, Inc.)*; (4) a requirement that a contract must be
ratified by a secret employee ballot *(NLRB v. Darlington Veneer
Co.)*; (5) a clause providing that a contract will become void
whenever more than 50 percent of the employees fail to
authorize dues checkoff *(NLRB v. Darlington Veneer Co.)*; (6) a
requirement that the union post a performance bond or an
indemnity bond to compensate the employer for losses caused
by picketing by other unions *(NLRB v. Taormina Co., Arlington
Asphalt Co.)*; (7) a requirement that employers post a cash bond
to cover any assessment for wages or fringe payments due under
the contract, or guarantee to pay to the union a sum equivalent
to the initiation fees the union would have received for each
employee not included in the bargaining unit if the employer
violated a clause barring subcontracting to employers not parties
to the master contract *(NLRB v. Hod Carriers Local 1082, NLRB v.
Bricklayers Local 3)*; (8) a clause fixing terms and conditions of
employment for workers hired to replace strikers *(Times Publish-
ing Co)*; (9) strike insurance obtained by employers to guard
against the financial risks involved in a strike *(Operating Engineers
Local 12)*; (10) benefits for retirees *(Chemical Workers v. Pittsburgh
Plate Glass Co.)*; (11) interest-arbitration clauses calling for arbitration of disputes over terms of a new contract *(NLRB v.
Columbus Printing Pressmen)*; (12) use of a court reporter to
transcribe negotiating sessions *(Bartlett-Collins Co.)*; (13) inclusion in a collective bargaining contract of a union "bug"
indicating that the contract was printed by union-represented
employees *(Electrical Workers (IBEW) Local 1464 (Kansas City Power*

& Light Co.)); (14) tape recording of grievance meetings *(NLRB v. Pennsylvania Telephone Guild)*; (15) promotion of employees to supervisory positions *(Pittsburgh Metal Processing Co., Inc.)*; (16) a no-strike clause under which employees would waive their right to seek redress from the NLRB for discipline imposed on strikers who are replaced. *(Reichhold Chemicals, Inc.)*

AUTHORITY, SELECTION OF NEGOTIATORS

There is no general rule on how much authority an employer or a union must vest in its negotiator in order to meet the good-faith bargaining obligation. The question has been handled by the NLRB and the courts on a case-by-case basis.

A negotiator must have sufficient authority for meaningful bargaining. *(NLRB v. Fitzgerald Mills Corp.)* Nothing in the Act requires a party to give a negotiator complete authority to reach an agreement, one court said, but the degree of authority given may be considered in determining whether there was good-faith bargaining. *(Lloyd A. Fry Roofing Co. v. NLRB)*

Attempts to dictate the choice of the other party's negotiators have been found unlawful. *(Wade & Paxton, NLRB v. Deena Artware, Inc., Iron Castings, Inc., NLRB v. Teamsters Local 294)* But refusals to meet with the other party's negotiator have been upheld in exceptional situations, as where a management negotiator previously held a highly confidential position in the union *(NLRB v. Garment Workers)* and where a union negotiator had "hostility" toward the employer and had said he wished to destroy the employer financially. *(NLRB v. Kentucky Utilities Co.)*

Generally, an employer who is bargaining for one unit may not refuse to meet with a union negotiating team merely because it includes representatives of other unions that have separate units of their own. *(American Radiator & Standard Sanitary Corp. v. NLRB, Minnesota Mining & Manufacturing Co. v. NLRB)* Courts have said that such refusals to meet may be justified, however, if it is shown that the presence of the "outsiders" represents a clear and present danger to the bargaining process *(General Electric Co. v. NLRB)* or that the unions are acting in bad faith or with an ulterior motive. *(Standard Oil Co. v. NLRB)* And an employer was found justified in refusing to bargain with a union negotiating committee that included representatives of other unions, where these other unions represented no employees of the employer but did represent the employees of his competitors. *(Electrical Workers (IBEW) v. NLRB)*

Conversely, an employer who had collective bargaining relationships with two different unions could not insist on the presence of representatives of both unions as a condition to meeting with either. *(F. W. Woolworth Co.)*

CONDUCT OF NEGOTIATIONS

The duty to bargain in good faith is defined in the Taft-Hartley Act as requiring the representatives of the employer and the union "to meet at reasonable times and confer in good faith with respect to wages, hours, and other terms and conditions of employment." It also requires the execution of a written contract incorporating any agreement reached if requested by either party. But it does not require either party to agree to a proposal or to make a concession.

The requirement that the parties meet at "reasonable times" does not mean a union representing 19 separate bargaining units could insist on the employer's meeting at a single time and place to bargain over revisions of companywide fringe benefit plans, despite a contention that single-unit bargaining on such plans was ineffective. *(Oil Workers v. NLRB; cf. AFL-CIO Joint Negotiating Committee v. NLRB)*

The NLRB and the courts have made it clear that merely going through the motions of bargaining is not enough. Violations of the Act have been found on the basis of a party's overall approach to and conduct of bargaining, including its behavior both at and away from the bargaining table. *(NLRB v. General Electric Co.)* Among the indicia of bad faith are a refusal to discuss or consider the other party's proposals *(Adler Metal Products Corp.)*, use of delaying tactics, with frequent postponements of bargaining sessions *(Rex Manufacturing Co., Inc.)*, and the withdrawal of concessions previously granted. *(Tomlinson of High Point, Inc.)*

The test is whether a party's attitude on the entire record indicates a good-faith desire to reach agreement with the other party. But this does not require "fruitless marathon discussions at the expense of frank statement and support of one's position." *(NLRB v. American National Insurance Co.)*

In some cases, the Board has indicated, specific proposals might become relevant in determining whether a party has bargained in bad faith. The Board will consider whether, on the basis of objective factors, a demand clearly is designed to frustrate agreement on a contract. *(Reichhold Chemicals, Inc.)* A party's unwillingness to enter into a contract for a fixed term raises the presumption that the party is not bargaining in good faith. *(Massillon Community Hospital)*

Lawful Tactics and Conduct

Examining each case on the basis of its own facts, the NLRB and the courts have found that a variety of tactics and conduct did not indicate a lack of good faith. Some examples are: (1) insisting on "uniformity" of wage and other items for a company's unionized and nonunionized employees *(Texas Foundries, Inc. v. NLRB)*, (2) refusing to offer a counterproposal in the face of an uncompromising position *(Old Line Life Insurance Co.)*, (3) insisting on a no-strike clause without an arbitration clause and on limiting membership on the grievance committee to plant employees *(NLRB v. Cummer-Graham Co.)*, (4) substantially adhering to a "final offer" in seven negotiating sessions *(Phillip Carey Manufacturing Co. v. NLRB)*, and (5) refusing to accept a predecessor employer's labor agreement as a starting point for negotiations. *(United States Gypsum Co. v. NLRB)*

The NLRB cleared one employer of charges of violating the bargaining duty, even though the bargaining covered 28 months and 74 formal negotiating sessions, and the employer communicated extensively with employees during the negotiations. The Board pointed to the company's willingness to make concessions and to its "fair and factual" communications with the employees. *(Procter & Gamble Manufacturing Co.)*

The Supreme Court held that a union's resort to unprotected harassing tactics—refusing to write new business during certain periods, to make reports as specified, to participate in conferences, etc.—as a means of putting pressure on the employer during bargaining did not amount to a violation of the bargaining duty. An employer may have the right to discipline the union members for such tactics, the Court said, but this does not make the tactics an unfair labor practice. *(NLRB v. Insurance Agents' International Union)*

Impasse

Once an employer has bargained to impasse, he may make unilateral changes "reasonably comprehended within his pre-impasse proposals." Whether an impasse exists is a matter of judgment requiring consideration of factors such as (1) bargaining history, (2) good faith in negotiations, (3) length of negotiations, (4) importance of the issues on which there is disagreement, and (5) the contemporaneous understanding of the parties as to the state of negotiations. *(Taft Broadcasting Co.)* Impasse may be reached after only a few bargaining sessions. *(Bell Transit Co.)*

DATA FOR BARGAINING

To meet his bargaining duty under the Act, an employer is required to furnish a union bargaining agent, on request, with sufficient data on wage rates, job classifications, and allied matters to permit the union to (1) bargain understandingly, (2) police the administration of the current contract, and (3) prepare for coming negotiations. The issues in such cases are whether the information sought is relevant to the union's obligations as bargaining agent, and if so, whether the information is sufficiently needed or important to invoke a statutory obligation to produce it. *(Columbus Products Co.)* A policy or practice of confidentiality cannot justify a per se refusal to furnish any information from personnel files; there must be a "more specific demonstration of a confidential interest in the particular information requested." *(Washington Gas Light Co.)*

The information an employer is required to furnish the union may cover a broad range of topics. Employers have been required, for example, to furnish the following, although it need not be in the exact form the union requests: arbitration claim files necessary to evaluate the employer's compliance with an award *(Twin City Lines, Inc.)*; information relating to the cost of proposed improvements in existing welfare programs *(Sylvania Electric Products, Inc. v. NLRB)*; wage and fringe benefit information for 16 classifications outside the bargaining unit *(General Electric Co.)*; information relating to the exact salaries paid employees in the unit, including salaries in excess of those specified in the union contract *(Cowles Communications, Inc.)*; time study and job evaluation data *(J. I. Case v. NLRB)*; dates of employment and seniority standing of individual employees *(NLRB v. Scharfstein)*; number of hours worked by individual employees *(F. W. Woolworth Co.)*; job classifications, job descriptions, wage rates, and rate ranges *(Dixie Corp.)*; production standards used in determining merit ratings *(Montgomery Ward & Co.)*; changes in productivity in the plant *(Hughes Tool Co.)*; pension and group insurance data *(NLRB v. Reed & Prince Manufacturing Co.)*; time studies and the employer's method of making them *(Otis Elevator Co.)*; information concerning the names of union officials who had applied for supervisory positions *(NLRB v. Postal Service)*; and a copy of a sales agreement in a case in which an employer had sold its newspapers. *(New England Newspapers, Inc.)*

On the question of time studies, the NLRB held in 1964 that a company was obligated to let a union make its own time studies of disputed operations. It found that the time studies were relevant and necessary to the union's administration of the grievance machinery of the contract and that the needed information was not available to the union through alternative channels. The decision was upheld by the U.S. Court of Appeals at New York. *(Fafnir Bearing Co. v. NLRB)* But the employer's right to control his property must be taken into account; a company is not required to open its doors merely because the presence of a union representative on company premises may be relevant to the union's performance of its duties. *(Holyoke Water Power Co.)*

Where geography and other circumstances make it extremely difficult for a union bargaining representative to communicate with members of the bargaining unit, the employer may be required to furnish the union with a list of the names and addresses of all employees in the unit represented by the union.

(Standard Oil Co. of California v. NLRB, Prudential Insurance Co. v. NLRB, United Aircraft Corp. v. NLRB)

Wage Data Obtained in Confidence

In a 1970 case, the NLRB held that a company that conducted an area wage survey violated the Act when it refused to furnish an incumbent union with correlated data tying job classifications and pay rates to the specific companies surveyed. The union challenged the data, but the company refused to reveal the companies from which the rates had been obtained, stating that they had been obtained in confidence. The Board rejected the company's position, stating that information is not exempt from disclosure merely because it was obtained in confidence. *(General Electric Co.)*

In a 1972 decision, the U.S. Court of Appeals in Cincinnati held that General Electric Co. violated the Act by refusing to disclose data obtained by wage surveys in four locations. The company was using the data in bargaining as a basis for refusing to raise wages at the plants. *(General Electric Co. v. NLRB)*

Data on Company's Financial Condition

If an employer pleads inability to meet a union's financial demands during negotiations, he also may be required to supply the union with financial data to back up his plea. But this obligation does not "automatically" follow a claim of inability to pay. It depends on the facts and circumstances of each case. Nor is the employer required to substantiate the claim; it is enough if he attempts to substantiate it. *(NLRB v. Truitt Manufacturing Co., Yakima Frozen Foods)* The same duty to provide substantiating data attaches to an employer who claims that competitive disadvantage precludes him from granting a wage increase. *(NLRB v. Western Wirebound Box Co.)*

An inability-to-pay claim need not be in "any particular magic words," so long as the employer's words and conduct are "specific enough to express such a meaning." *(Atlanta Hilton)* But employers who stated they needed "take-backs" to narrow the cost gap between union and nonunion wages and benefits did not raise a claim of inability to pay. *(Washington Materials v. NLRB)* Neither did employers who stated they could lose money and go out of business if their competitive positions did not improve. *(NLRB v. Harvstone Manufacturing Corp.)*

Health and Safety Data; Trade Secrets

A union was not entitled to the names of employees who had been "red tagged" because they had lung disease, the NLRB held, citing the "legitimate aura of confidentiality in the identities of those individuals who have been identified as having a certain medical disorder." The Board added that the union had other means of protecting employee interests and that the employer had sought to accommodate the union. *(Johns-Manville Sales Corp.)*

But employers have been ordered to give unions statistical or aggregate medical data even if this results in the unavoidable identification of some individual employee medical information. *(Minnesota Mining & Manufacturing Co., Colgate-Palmolive Co., Oil Workers v. NLRB)* The Board also held that the Privacy Act, which generally forbids government contractors to disclose information pertaining to an individual without his express authorization, did not bar the release of health and safety data to a union that promised to keep such information confidential and that sought statistical, aggregate data—not the unabridged, personal medical records of employees. *(Goodyear Atomic Corp.)*

If a union asserts that health and safety reasons entitle it to a list of generic names of substances used or produced in company plants, may the employer withhold the list on the ground that the names constitute "trade secrets"? The NLRB has said that the parties should initially bargain to establish conditions for the furnishing of the names under appropriate safeguards protecting the employer's legitimate interests. If the parties cannot reach satisfactory agreement, the Board said, it would then resolve the matter by balancing the union's right to relevant bargaining data against the employer's concerns regarding confidentiality. *(Minnesota Mining & Manufacturing Co., Colgate-Palmolive Co., Borden Chemical)* An appeals court agreed. *(Oil Workers Local 6-418 v. NLRB)*

In determining whether an incumbent union is entitled to enter a plant to survey potential health and safety hazards, the company's right to control its property is accommodated with the employees' right to proper representation. The employer's property rights will prevail where the union has alternate means of carrying out its duties. Even when the union is found entitled to access, such access will be limited to reasonable periods to avoid interruption of the employer's operations. (*Holyoke Water Power Co.*)

A mine operator unlawfully refused to give a union photographs of a mine site where an employee was killed, but the operator was not required to provide the union with its internal report on the accident. Access to the report and the employer's self-critical thinking was not found to be relevant to the union's representative duties. (*Asarco, Inc. v. NLRB*)

No-Discrimination Clauses

The NLRB has held that unions whose collective bargaining contracts contain no-discrimination clauses are entitled to (1) statistical data on minority groups and female unit employees; (2) copies of charges and complaints against the employer involving unit employees and filed under state and federal fair employment practice laws; (3) copies of work force analyses contained in affirmative action plans that the employer, as a government contractor, was required to develop; (4) information as to the race and sex of job applicants. But the unions were not entitled to copies of the affirmative action plans themselves, copies of FEP charges and complaints involving nonunit employees, and statistical data on nonunit female and minority group employees. (*Westinghouse Electric Corp., East Dayton Tool & Die Co., Minnesota Mining & Manufacturing Co.*)

An appeals court found that the Board's position on FEP charges and complaints of unit employees did not sufficiently ensure confidentiality. The Board had ordered copies of these furnished with names deleted, but the court said the employer need furnish only a compilation of the numbers, types, dates, and alleged bases of such charges and complaints. (*Electrical Workers (IUE) v. NLRB*)

Limits on Union Rights

An employer who used a psychological testing program in filling job openings met his statutory obligation when he offered to disclose test scores linked with employee names only if the examinees consented in writing, the U.S. Supreme Court held. A union's bare assertion that it needs information to process a grievance does not automatically require the employer to supply all the information in the manner requested, the Court said; the duty to supply information and the type of disclosure that will satisfy that duty turn on the circumstances of the particular case. *(Detroit Edison Co. v. NLRB)*

Employers have been upheld in insisting that any audit of company books be done in their office and by a licensed or certified public accountant *(Fruit Packers v. NLRB)*, in refusing to permit a union to take job evaluation and job description records out of the plant for study and analysis *(American Cyanamid Co.)*, and in refusing to furnish data that would be unduly burdensome to compile. *(Westinghouse Electric Corp.)*

Data to which unions have been found not entitled include, for example, point information used in evaluating the various elements of a job for classification purposes *(Anaconda American Brass Co.)*, information relating to the cost of a noncontributory group insurance program *(Sylvania Electric Products, Inc. v. NLRB)*, cost information relating to the subcontracting of certain work *(Southwestern Bell Telephone Co., Western Massachusetts Electric Co. v. NLRB)*, witness statements that an employer obtained in investigating alleged misconduct that had resulted in an employee's suspension and in his filing of a grievance *(Anheuser-Busch, Inc.)*, and security officers' written statements concerning strikers' alleged picket-line misconduct. *(Certainteed Corp.)*

A newspaper publisher was not required to give a union the names of employees who had been cross-trained in the operation of printing presses, a federal appeals court held, even assuming this information was presumptively relevant for bargaining. The union had received similar information earlier, the court noted, and instead of using it for bargaining purposes, it had posted the employees' names and termed them "scabs." *(NLRB v. A. S. Abell Co.; see also Shell Oil Co. v. NLRB)*

Data From Union

Assuming "without deciding" that a union's duty to furnish information relevant to the bargaining process is parallel to that of an employer, the NLRB nevertheless found that a union was not required to furnish an employer certain documents that the union claimed were in its possession and would win a forthcoming arbitration. *(Machinists Lodge 78)* But a violation of the bargaining duty was found where a union failed to provide an employer with information concerning trust fund contributions, to make reasonable efforts to obtain the information, to investigate reasonable alternative means of obtaining it, or to explain or document the reasons for the unavailability of the information. *(NLRB v. Retail, Wholesale and Department Store Union District 1199E)* The Board also found a violation where a union, during contract negotiations, refused to give an employer certain information concerning union rules and policies on the referral of employees *(Printing & Graphic Communications Union v. NLRB)* and where a union refused to give employers a list of names and addresses of persons subject to referral through an exclusive hiring hall. *(Electrical Workers (IBEW) Local 497 (Apple City Electric))*

Photocopies

Sound policy dictates that data relevant to bargaining should generally be furnished by photocopy, the NLRB has held, finding that reading documents to union representatives and permitting them to copy employer records did not satisfy the obligation to bargain. The employer was directed to give the union photocopies of the required records or let the union make the photocopies itself; the "reasonable additional costs" of such photocopying were to be determined through bargaining and were to be borne by the union. *(American Telephone & Telegraph Co., Communications Workers Local 1051 v. NLRB)* No photocopy was required, however, where the employer offered to let the union examine and take notes on the material sought—a single-page letter that could be understood in minutes. *(Roadway Express)*

WITHDRAWAL FROM MULTIEMPLOYER UNIT

The rules governing withdrawals from multiemployer units are the same for employers and for unions. *(Publishers' Association v. NLRB, Detroit Newspaper Publishers v. NLRB)* The withdrawal must be made before the date set for multiemployer negotiations, and the withdrawal must be unequivocal. *(Retail Associates, Inc.)*

Absent unusual circumstances, any untimely attempt of an employer to withdraw from multiemployer bargaining without the consent of the union and the multiemployer group is an unfair labor practice. An impasse in the multiemployer negotiations is not an "unusual circumstance" justifying withdrawal. *(Teamsters Local 378, Bonanno Linen Service v. NLRB)*

An employer's participation in multiemployer bargaining amounts to implicit recognition of the union and obligates the employer to continue recognizing the union even after the employer withdraws from the multiemployer group. *(NLRB v. Tahoe Nugget, Inc., NLRB v. Roger's I.G.A., Inc,; cf. NLRB v. Kaase Baking Co.)* But a union cannot be compelled to bargain individually with employers who have withdrawn from multiemployer bargaining. *(NLRB v. Plumbers Local 44)*

A union may withdraw from the multiemployer unit with respect to one or more employers, while continuing multiemployer bargaining with the remainder. The remaining employers also may withdraw if they feel that the union's fragmenting efforts make multiemployer bargaining no longer desirable. *(Pacific Coast Association of Pulp & Paper Manufacturers)* But after an impasse in the multiemployer negotiations, the union may negotiate interim agreements with individual members of the multiemployer group, without thereby creating new withdrawal rights in the remaining employers. *(Bonanno Linen Service)*

An employer may withdraw only part of his operations from a multiemployer unit, if the withdrawal is timely and for valid economic reasons. *(North American Refractories Co.)*

SUCCESSOR EMPLOYERS

For a number of years, there was considerable controversy about the collective bargaining obligations of a company that acquired a business from another company having a contract or an established bargaining relationship with a union. In a landmark decision handed down in 1972, the Supreme Court laid down these rules:

- A successor employer who retains the employees of the predecessor employer is required to bargain with the union that represents a majority of the employees.
- The successor employer is not, however, required to honor the contract that the predecessor negotiated with the union.
- If a successor employer clearly intends to retain all of his predecessor's employees, he may be required to consult the union before setting terms of employment; but this is not so where the successor's bargaining duty becomes clear only after his full employee complement has been hired. (*NLRB v. Burns International Security Services; see also NLRB v. Spruce Up Corp., Vantage Petroleum Corp.*)

Subsequently, the Court held that an employer who acquires and operates in basically unchanged form the business of an employer found guilty of unfair labor practices, under circumstances that charge the purchaser with notice of the unfair labor practice charges against the seller, will be jointly and severally liable with the seller for remedying the unfair labor practices. (*Golden State Bottling Co. v. NLRB*)

In another ruling on successor employers, the Supreme Court expanded on its *Burns International* decision. When a union that was certified for more than one year has a rebuttable presumption of majority status, that status continues despite a change in employers, the Court ruled. Although the successor employer is not bound by the substantive provisions of its predecessor's bargaining agreement, it is obligated to bargain with the union so long as it is in fact the successor of the old employer and the majority of its employees were employed by its predecessor.

The Court found reasonable the NLRB's "substantial and representative" complement rule, under which the successor employer's obligation to bargain is determined as of the time its job classifications are substantially filled and its operation is in normal production. It also approved the Board's "continuing demand" rule, under which a union's premature demand for bargaining continues in effect until the successor employer acquires a substantial and representative complement of employees, triggering its bargaining obligation. (*Fall River Dyeing & Finishing Corp. v. NLRB*)

A franchiser that purchased the assets of a restaurant and motor lodge and hired only a small fraction of the seller's employees was not required to arbitrate the extent of its obligations under the seller's collective bargaining contract to the seller's employees whom it did not hire. This was a Supreme Court decision. (*Howard Johnson Co. v. Detroit Joint Board*) The decision limits the scope of the *John Wiley* decision in which the Court held that the obligation to arbitrate disputes survived both the expiration of the contract and the disappearance of the corporate employer by merger.

FAIR REPRESENTATION

It has been held under both the Railway Labor Act and the Taft-Hartley Act that a union must represent all members of the bargaining unit without invidious discrimination. The Supreme Court has ruled that a breach of this duty of fair representation occurs when a union's conduct with respect to a member of the bargaining unit is arbitrary, discriminatory, or in bad faith. The NLRB regards a breach of the duty of fair representation as an unfair labor practice (*NLRB v. Miranda Fuel Co.*), but the Court said that this fact does not bar state or federal courts from taking an employee's action against a union for breach of the duty of fair representation. (*Vaca v. Sipes*)

A union that handles an apparently meritorious discharge grievance in a perfunctory and arbitrary manner may be held primarily liable for part of the wages and benefits lost by the discharged employee. (*Bowen v. United States Postal Service*) But punitive damages are not recoverable in actions for breach of the duty of fair representation. (*Electrical Workers (IBEW) v. Foust*)

The remedial machinery of the Taft-Hartley Act is not available to a union that practices racial discrimination, a federal appeals court said, holding that an employer could introduce evidence of a union's racially discriminatory practices as a defense to a refusal-to-bargain charge. *(NLRB v. Mansion House Corp.)* In the view of the NLRB, however, discrimination by a union on racial or other invidious grounds should not bar its certification, but the certification may be revoked if it is established in a subsequent unfair labor practice proceeding that the union does in fact engage in invidious discrimination. *(Handy Andy, Inc., Bell & Howell Co. v. NLRB)*

MAKE-WHOLE REMEDIES

One of the problems in refusal-to-bargain cases is whether the NLRB has authority to issue "make-whole" orders requiring an employer to reimburse employees retroactively for increased wages and fringe benefits the employees would have received had the employer bargained in good faith.

In the leading *H.K. Porter* case, the Supreme Court held that the NLRB has no authority to compel an employer or a union to agree to any substantive provision of a collective bargaining contract. Specifically, the Court held that the Board had no authority to order a company to agree to a dues checkoff, even though the Court upheld the Board's finding that the company had not bargained in good faith.

Despite *H.K. Porter*, it has been held that the NLRB has authority to issue a make-whole order to give meaningful relief to employees unlawfully denied the fruits of collective bargaining. *(Electrical Workers (IUE) v. NLRB, Steelworkers v. NLRB; see NLRB v. Food Store Employees Local 347)* The Board has said, however, that such a compensatory remedy can be provided only by Congress. *(Ex-Cell-O Corp. v. NLRB)*

In a case in which a union unlawfully refused to execute a three-year collective bargaining contract, the Board had authority to order the union to execute the contract with its specified expiration date but not to extend the contract so as to give the employer the benefit of a full three-year contract. *(Hyatt Management Corp. v. NLRB)*

6

LAWFUL AND UNLAWFUL UNION-SECURITY CLAUSES

There are a number of types of union-security clauses. The following are the principal ones:

- *Closed Shop*. These clauses require that the employer hire only members of a particular union. Closed-shop contracts are illegal under the Taft-Hartley Act.

- *Full Union Shop*. Under these clauses an employer may hire an employee who is not a member of the union but all employees must join the union within a specified period of time, usually 30 days after hiring.

- *Modified Union Shop*. The most common form of modified union shop requires new employees to join the union and present employees and all who join to maintain their union membership. However, old employees who are not members of the union may continue to stay out of the union.

- *Maintenance of Membership*. These clauses require persons who become union members to continue their membership, but they do not impose any membership requirement on other employees.

- *Agency Shop*. These clauses obligate employees who do not join the union to pay the equivalent of union dues and fees for the union's services.

The Supreme Court, ruling on agency-shop provisions, has held:

- The Railway Labor Act does not permit a union, over the objection of nonmembers, to expend compelled agency fees on political causes. *(Machinists v. Street)*
- A union may not over the objection of an agency-fee payer expend agency-fee funds on activities beyond those germane to collective bargaining, contract administration, and grievance adjustment. *(Communications Workers v. Beck)*
- The First Amendment requires that a public-sector union that imposes an agency-shop fee on non-members adequately explain the basis for the fee, provide a reasonably prompt opportunity to challenge the amount of the fee before an impartial decision-maker, and establish an escrow for reasonably disputed amounts while challenges are pending. *(Chicago Teachers Union Local 1 v. Hudson)*

Hiring Arrangements

The use of union hiring halls as employment agencies has been a common practice in industries where employment is casual or intermittent, such as the construction and longshoring industries. A union may charge nonmembers a fee to help pay the expenses of a hiring hall *(Pacific Maritime Association)*, but the fee cannot be equal to the dues paid by union members. *(NLRB v. Operating Engineers Local 138)*

TAFT-HARTLEY RESTRICTIONS

Under the Taft-Hartley Act, it is an unfair labor practice for an employer to discriminate against an employee or applicant for employment either because he is a member of a union or because he is not a member of a union. It also is an unfair labor practice for a union to cause an employer to so discriminate.

A proviso to Section 8(a)(3), however, permits an employer and a union to agree to a limited form of union shop. If a union is the majority bargaining agent, it may sign a union-shop contract subject to the following conditions:

- Membership may be required only after 30 days following the effective date of the contract or the beginning of employment, whichever is later.
- The union must admit eligible employees to membership without discrimination, although the union retains the right to make its own rules of eligibility.
- When a union-shop contract has been made under these conditions, the union may seek an employee's discharge for non-membership only when membership has been withdrawn for failure to tender an initiation fee or the periodic dues.

Under a 1974 amendment to the Taft-Hartley Act, health care institution employees whose religion barred them from joining or supporting a labor organization were exempted from union-security clauses but could be required to pay the equivalent of union dues or fees to one of three nonreligious charitable funds listed in the collective bargaining contract. In 1980, this provision was extended to all employees covered by the Act, not just employees of health care institutions.

The "membership" that may be required under a union-security arrangement is "financial core" membership—the payment of union dues and fees. An employee may not be required to become a full member of the union. (*NLRB v. General Motors, NLRB v. Hershey Foods Corp.*)

A union seeking to enforce a union-security contract against an employee has a fiduciary duty to treat him fairly. It must inform him of his obligations, so that he has a chance to take whatever action is necessary to protect his job. (*NLRB v. Hotel Employees Local 568, Machinists Lodge 946*)

Exceptions for Construction Industry

The 1959 amendments to the Act established some special union-security rules for the building and construction industry. These rules permit a building trades employer to make a prehire, union-shop contract with a construction union under these conditions:

- The contract may be executed before the majority status of the union has been established under the Act.
- The contract may require employees to join the union seven days after their employment or after the effective date of the contract, whichever is later.
- The contract may require the employer to notify the union of job opportunities and to give the union an opportunity to refer qualified applicants.
- The agreement may specify minimum training or experience qualifications for employment or provide for priority in opportunities for employment based upon length of service with the employer, in the industry, or in the geographical area.

A prehire agreement binds both parties during its term, but either may repudiate the prehire relationship once the agreement expires, and the signatory union may not strike or picket for a successor prehire agreement. *(Iron Workers Local 3 v. NLRB (Deklewa & Sons))*

It is not clear whether a signatory union may picket to protest an employer's unlawful repudiation of a prehire contract. *(Deklewa & Sons, NLRB v. Iron Workers Local 103 (Higdon Contracting Co.), City Electric)*

Monetary obligations that an employer assumes pursuant to a prehire agreement may be recovered by a union, even if it has not achieved majority status, in a suit brought before the employer repudiates the contract. *(McNeff, Inc. v. Todd)*

CHECKOFF

Checkoff arrangements, under which the employer deducts union dues from employee wages and remits them to the union, are permitted under the Taft-Hartley Act. But an employee has the right to refuse to sign a checkoff authorization *(American Screw Co.)*, and the Act provides that a checkoff authorization cannot be made irrevocable for more than a year or beyond the expiration date of the contract, whichever occurs first.

Federal appeals courts have said that this provision of the Act gives employees the right to revoke their checkoff authorizations at the expiration of each collective bargaining contract (*Office & Professional Employees Local 42 v. Auto Workers Local 174*), even though the authorizations themselves provide that revocations must be made between 60 and 75 days before the anniversary date of the checkoff authorization, or the date the contract expires. (*Anheuser-Busch, Inc. v. Teamsters Local 822*)

The NLRB's view is that expiration of the contract makes checkoff authorizations revocable at will if such an intention is evident from the authorizations or from the applicable contract, but if the checkoff authorizations themselves limit revocability, employees may not revoke them merely because no contract is in effect. (*Frito-Lay, Inc.*)

Where a checkoff authorization provided that it was given in consideration of benefits received as a result of union membership, the Board held that resignation from membership revoked the checkoff authorization by operation of law. (*San Diego County District Council of Carpenters*)

UNION-SHOP DEAUTHORIZATION ELECTIONS

Suppose employees in a unit covered by a valid union-shop contract decide they no longer want a union shop. The NLRB will conduct a union-shop deauthorization election. A petition for such an election may be filed by 30 percent of the employees in the unit or by an employee or group acting on behalf of them. The usual contract-bar rules do not apply to such petitions, although the unit must be the same as that covered by the contract. If a majority of the employees *eligible to vote*, not merely those who cast ballots, vote for deauthorization, the union-shop clause is suspended. If an election results in a union-shop deauthorization, an employer may violate the Act by continuing to honor "irrevocable" check-off authorizations. (*NLRB v. Penn Cork & Closures, Inc.*)

STATE RIGHT-TO-WORK LAWS

Under Section 14(b) of the Taft-Hartley Act, there is a specific sanction for state laws that regulate union security more strictly than does the federal Act. In line with this sanction, 21 states have so-called right-to-work laws aimed at outlawing most, if not all, forms of union security. These 21 states are: Alabama, Arizona, Arkansas, Florida, Georgia, Idaho, Iowa, Kansas, Louisiana, Mississippi, Nebraska, Nevada, North Carolina, North Dakota, South Carolina, South Dakota, Tennessee, Texas, Utah, Virginia, and Wyoming.

The constitutionality of such laws was upheld by the U.S. Supreme Court in 1949. *(Lincoln Union v. Northwestern Iron & Metal Co., AFL v. American Sash & Door Co.)* The agency shop, under which nonmembers have to pay the equivalent of union dues, has been held unlawful under the right-to-work laws of most of the states. In three decisions handed down in 1963, the Supreme Court held that an agency shop is lawful under the Taft-Hartley Act, but added that the states have the authority to outlaw agency-shop contracts under the sanction provided by Section 14(b) of the Taft-Hartley Act. A state thus may declare such a contract illegal and enjoin its enforcement. *(NLRB v. General Motors, Retail Clerks Local 1625 v. Schermerhorn)*

In describing the effect of Section 14(b), the Supreme Court said that Congress left the states free to legislate in the field of union-security agreements, and it did not deprive them of the power to enforce their laws restricting the execution and enforcement of such agreements. But the state power recognized in Section 14(b) begins only with the actual negotiation and enforcement of the union-security agreement. So picketing to obtain union-security agreements remains within the exclusive jurisdiction of the NLRB, while the states have the power to declare a contract illegal and enjoin its enforcement, including ordering reinstatement with back pay of an employee discharged under a contract that violates the state law. *(Retail Clerks Local 1625 v. Schermerhorn)*

The Texas right-to-work laws did not govern the validity of an agency-shop agreement covering seamen who performed most of their work on the high seas, the Supreme Court held, even though Texas may have had more contacts than any other state with the employment relationship between the seamen and their employer. If the predominant job situs is outside the boundaries of any state, then no state has a sufficient interest in the employment relationship to make its right-to-work laws applicable, the Court said. *(Oil Workers v. Mobil Oil Corp.)*

In a case placing a limitation on right-to-work laws, an appeals court held that a hiring-hall arrangement expressly stating that union membership is not to be considered in job referrals is not subject to state regulation under a right-to-work law. Although Section 14(b) permits right-to-work laws, it does not protect a state law that is so broadly stated or construed as to bar such nondiscriminatory hiring-hall arrangements. *(NLRB v. Tom Joyce Floors, Inc.)*

7

STRIKES, PICKETING, BOYCOTTS, AND LOCKOUTS

In the background of every labor controversy is the possibility of a strike by the employees or a lockout by the employer. These are the ultimate weapons of industrial strife when negotiations break down.

The concerted stoppage of work known as a strike, however, may be of little effect in enforcing the workers' demands if the employer is able to replace the strikers and resume normal production. To prevent such an outcome, unions customarily resort to picketing. They also may resort to picketing as a means of exerting pressure on an employer from whom they are seeking recognition as a bargaining agent.

In its simplest form, picketing is merely a type of advertising. It informs the public—and other workers—that there is a strike or dispute and states the union's version of its cause. But if feelings run high, the picketing may take the form of persuading customers not to patronize the employer or other employees not to enter the employer's premises.

Closely tied in with strikes and picketing is the boycott. A simple or primary boycott is a refusal to deal with, patronize, or permit union members to work for an employer with whom the union has a dispute. At times, however, the union finds it more effective to act against the customers or suppliers of the target employer. The boycott then becomes a secondary boycott. The union may set up a picket line at the premises of the customers or suppliers—the neutral or secondary employers.

THE LABOR INJUNCTION

For many years, the usual response of an employer to picketing and boycotts was to go into court and obtain an injunction against the union. But in 1932, Congress adopted the Norris-LaGuardia Act forbidding the federal courts to issue injunctions in labor disputes unless certain prior conditions are fulfilled. A number of the states then adopted "little Norris-La-Guardia acts" patterned after the federal law.

Among the conditions that must be fulfilled before an injunction may be issued is that the union be given an opportunity to state its case; there may be no ex parte injunctions. A showing also must be made that all efforts to obtain a settlement by conciliation and other methods provided for by law have been exhausted and that the withholding of the injunction will cause more harm to one party than granting it will cause to the other party.

An exception to the law was made when the Supreme Court held that the government might obtain an injunction against a strike directed at it as an employer operating an industrial property. An injunction issued against a strike of the coal mines at a time when they were being operated by the government was upheld by the Court. *(United States v. Mine Workers)*

The adoption in 1947 of the Taft-Hartley Act established a detailed federal code of law governing strikes, picketing, and boycotts. Additions were made to this code by the 1959 Landrum-Griffin amendments to the law.

TAFT-HARTLEY RESTRICTIONS

The Taft-Hartley Act specifically restricts the right to strike and to picket in several important respects. Section 8(b)(4) makes it an unfair labor practice for a union or its agents to engage in or encourage a strike for any one of the following purposes:

- Forcing any employer or self-employed person to join a labor or employer organization or to enter into a hot-cargo contract. This is directed mainly against certain types of secondary boycotts.

- Forcing any person to cease doing business with any other person. This is the so-called secondary boycott.
- Forcing an employer other than the one employing the union's members to recognize as bargaining agent any union not certified by the NLRB. This is the so-called secondary recognition strike.
- Forcing an employer to recognize a union as bargaining agent if another union already has been certified to represent his employees.
- Forcing an employer to transfer work from one group of employees to another group. This includes so-called work jurisdiction or work task picketing.

RECOGNITION PICKETING

Section 8(b)(7) inserted in the Taft-Hartley Act by the 1959 amendments makes it unlawful for a union to picket "to force or require" the employer to recognize the union or the employees to accept it as bargaining agent where:

- Another union has been recognized as bargaining agent, and the NLRB would not conduct an election because a question of representation does not exist.
- A valid election has been conducted within the preceding 12 months.
- The picketing has been conducted for a reasonable period of time (not to exceed 30 days), and no election petition has been filed.

Sanctions Provided

Strikes and picketing for the purposes mentioned above not only are made unfair labor practices but also are subject to special sanctions. Except with respect to work task picketing, the NLRB's General Counsel is required to seek a federal court injunction against continuance of the strike or picketing if he believes that a formal unfair labor practice proceeding should be commenced by the issuance of a complaint. For work task picketing and other types of unfair labor practices, the General

Counsel has discretion with respect to seeking an injunction. The injunction ordinarily runs until the NLRB has issued a decision in the case.

In addition, any person injured by any of the enumerated types of strikes and picketing may sue for damages in the federal courts. This right is not granted by the Taft-Hartley Act with respect to other types of union conduct involving strikes and picketing, even though the conduct may involve unfair labor practices.

PUBLICIZING DISPUTE

Both the secondary boycott prohibition and the provisions restricting recognition and organizational picketing contain provisos designed to preserve a union's right to publicize a dispute with an employer. The proviso in the secondary boycott prohibition states that nothing in the provision should be construed to bar a union from using publicity for the purpose of "truthfully advising" the public, consumers, and union members that the neutral employer is distributing goods produced by an employer with whom the union has a dispute.

The publicity proviso in the recognition picketing section is attached to the provision making it unlawful to picket for recognition or organizational purposes where no election petition is filed within a reasonable period of time. The proviso permits both picketing and other publicity for the purpose of truthfully advising the public of the dispute unless the effect is to stop deliveries or performance of services by employees of other employers.

Dual-Purpose Picketing

One of the first questions raised under the restrictions on recognition and organizational picketing was whether picketing that had a dual purpose—recognition and publicity—was prohibited. Reversing its initial interpretations of the provisions, the NLRB laid down these rules:

- Purely informational picketing is not barred under any of the three subsections of Section 8(b)(7). To be subject to the ban, the picketing must have recognition or organization as an object. Thus, a union may engage in purely informational picketing without regard to whether another union has been lawfully recognized or a valid election has been conducted within the last 12 months, or if no election petition was filed within a reasonable period of time.

- If picketing is purely informational, it is immaterial that it stops pickups or deliveries. This would not make it unlawful.

- Dual-purpose picketing—that which has both information and recognition as objects—comes within the protection of the proviso to subparagraph (C). It becomes unlawful only if it stops pickups or deliveries. *(Hotel & Restaurant Employees Local 681)*

- *Moreover,* minor interference with pickups or deliveries will not make the picketing unlawful. The picketing will be unlawful only if it has "disrupted, interfered with, or curtailed the employer's business." *(Retail Clerks Locals 324 and 770, Barker Brothers Corp. v. NLRB)* However, picketing that is a "signal" to organized labor to stop work does not come within the protection of the proviso and is unlawful even though it does not stop deliveries or services. *(Electrical Workers (IBEW) Local 3)*

Although picketing to protect area labor standards does not come within the restriction on recognition picketing, picketing to compel an employer to sign a contract to pay wages and fringes equal to those paid under union contracts is recognition picketing subject to the Section 8(b)(7) restrictions. *(Houston Building & Construction Trades Council, Centralia Building & Construction Trades Council v. NLRB)* In cases that appear to involve area standards picketing, the Board often is concerned with the truth of the union's assertion that the picketed employer paid substandard wages and fringes, since if the statement is not true, there could be a possible inference of some other object. *(Plumbers Local 614)*

Picketing to obtain the reinstatement of a discharged employee is not necessarily picketing to compel recognition or bargaining. *(Auto Workers Local 259)*

SCOPE OF BOYCOTT BAN

Prior to the 1959 amendments to the Act, the scope of the secondary boycott ban was quite limited. To establish a violation of the ban, it was necessary to show that the union induced or encouraged employees of a neutral employer to strike or refuse to perform services as a means of putting pressure on the neutral employer to stop doing business with a struck employer. There was nothing unlawful in a union's going directly to the neutral employer and by threats or other means getting him to stop doing business with the struck employer.

The 1959 amendments sought to close this loophole with new language. A somewhat broadened version of the old provision bars inducement or encouragement of individuals employed by neutral employers to strike or refuse to perform services. A new provision makes it unlawful for a union to use threats, coercion, or restraint to compel any "person"—a term that includes an employer—to stop doing business with another. Thus, it no longer is lawful for a union to effectuate a secondary boycott by putting pressure directly on a neutral employer or his managerial employees by threats, coercion, or restraint to exercise their managerial discretion to stop doing business with the struck employer. *(NLRB v. Servette, Inc.)*

A key Supreme Court decision held that if a union directs appeals to managerial employees of a neutral employer who does business with a struck employer, the appeals will violate the secondary boycott provisions only if they are to induce the employees to withhold their services from their employer with an object of forcing him to stop doing business with the struck employer. If the appeals are to induce the employees to exercise their "managerial discretion" to stop doing business with the struck employer, they will violate the Act only if they threaten, coerce, or restrain the employees in the exercise of their managerial discretion. *(NLRB v. Servette, Inc.)*

In addition to closing the loophole relating to threats, coercion, or restraint directed at the employer himself, the 1959 amendments made these additional changes:

- Unions were prohibited from inducing individual employees one at a time to engage in secondary boycotts.
- The boycott ban was extended to inducements of supervisors, farm labor, railroads, municipalities, and government agencies. The ban also applies to threats, coercion, or restraint of railroads, municipalities, or government agencies.

BOYCOTTS: PUBLICITY PROVISO

In an authorization for consumer appeals at retail stores, the 1959 amendments stated that nothing in the secondary boycott provisions shall be construed to prohibit a union from using publicity for the purpose of truthfully advising the public, consumers, and members of unions that goods are produced by an employer with whom the union has a dispute and are distributed by another employer. But two important conditions were attached:

- First, the union may not picket the neutral establishment.
- Second, the publicity may not induce employees of neutral employers to refuse to pick up, deliver, or transport any goods or to refuse to perform any services at the distributor's establishment.

The proviso, the Supreme Court ruled, is not limited to disputes in which the struck employer is a manufacturer. It applies, for example, to a wholesaler or distributor. (*NLRB v. Servette, Inc.*) It also applies to a television station as the "producer" of the products advertised on its programs. (*Television & Radio Artists*)

Handbilling

But the Supreme Court found that the proviso did not apply to union handbills urging consumers not to patronize any of the stores in a shopping center where a department store was being built by a contractor with whom the union had a dispute. (*Edward J. DeBartolo Corp. v. NLRB*)

Although the Court found that the handbilling in *DeBartolo* was not protected by the publicity proviso, the Court later held that this picketing was lawful despite the statutory prohibition of secondary boycotts. Construing the statute so as to avoid the First Amendment issue, the Court found no clear indication of a congressional intent to proscribe peaceful handbilling, unaccompanied by picketing, that urges a consumer boycott of a neutral employer. (*Edward J. DeBartolo Corp. v. Florida Gulf Coast Building & Constr. Trades Council*)

DeBartolo involved pure handbilling. Finding that a union coercively attempted to discourage use of a club house on which a nonunion general contractor was working, an appeals court said that handbilling that is part of a course of conduct that includes picketing and blocking the approach of patrons is unlawful. (*Boxhorn's Big Muskego Gun Club v. Electrical Workers (IBEW) Local 494*)

Another appeals court has found that a union that had a labor dispute with a television station lawfully distributed, at entrances to stores that advertised on the station, handbills urging a consumer boycott of the stores. The union's actions in writing letters to, telephoning, and visiting the stores to warn them of the union's impending handbilling were also lawful. (*Storer Communications, Inc. v. National Association of Broadcast Employees and Technicians*)

The Board applied *DeBartolo* to find lawful a union's handbilling and other nonpicketing activity urging a consumer boycott of all products and services of a conglomerate and its divisions and subsidiaries, even if the divisions and subsidiaries were neutral parties. (*Steelworkers*)

Object of Picketing

Although the publicity proviso of the secondary boycott provisions clearly forbids picketing of the retail stores, the Supreme Court ruled that it does not forbid *all* peaceful picketing of the stores. It only bars picketing to persuade customers to stop trading with the stores to force them to stop dealing with the struck employer. Picketing merely to persuade customers not to purchase the products of the struck employer is closely confined to the primary dispute and is not forbidden. *(NLRB v. Fruit Packers Local 760)*

But picketing ostensibly directed at a struck employer's product was unlawful where it left responsive consumers no realistic option other than to boycott the neutral employers altogether, the Supreme Court later held, finding a secondary boycott violation by a union that was striking an insurance underwriter and that picketed five title companies deriving more than 90 percent of their income from the sale of the underwriter's insurance. *(NLRB v. Retail Clerks Local 1001)*

The Court noted that situations may arise in which a secondary boycott is directed against a product representing a "major portion" of a neutral's business but "significantly less than that represented by a single dominant product." In such cases, the Court said, the question for the NLRB is whether, by encouraging customers to reject the struck product, the secondary appeal is reasonably likely to threaten the neutral party with ruin or substantial loss.

The struck product must be clearly identified, an appeals court said, and the picketing must not be aimed at inducing a general loss of business at the picketed store. So a broad appeal "to look for the union label" was found to be an unlawful secondary boycott. *(Furniture Workers Local 140 v. NLRB)*

A union also was held to have violated the secondary boycott ban by picketing a shopping center in an attempt to induce customers not to patronize four restaurants and one jewelry store that advertised in a newspaper with which the union had a dispute. The union's object was to force the restaurants and the store to stop advertising in the newspaper. Since the restaurants and the store advertised their entire businesses, not just their products, the picketing amounted to more than the mere following of a struck product. *(Honolulu Typographical Union v. NLRB)*

Under the "merged product" doctrine, picketing that purports to follow a struck product is unlawful where this product has become an integral part of a retailer's entire operation. Thus, a union unlawfully picketed a restaurant in furtherance of a labor dispute with the producer of the bread the restaurant served with meals. *(American Bread Co. v. NLRB)*

Common-Situs Picketing

Some of the most difficult cases under the secondary boycott ban have been those involving picketing on a work site at which employees both of the struck employer and of neutral employers are working. The NLRB has established these tests for the legality of such common-situs picketing:

- Picketing must be limited to times when the struck employer's employees actually are present at the common site.
- Picketing must be limited to places "reasonably close" to the operations of the struck employer's workers.
- The pickets must show clearly that their dispute is with the struck employer alone.
- The struck employer's workers must be engaged in the employer's normal business. *(Sailors' Union of the Pacific)*

The NLRB has stressed, however, that these tests are not the sole guide for determining the legality of common-situs picketing. They are rather evidentiary in nature, and they are to be applied in the absence of more direct evidence of the intent and purpose of the union. The mere compliance with the four requirements does not immunize a union from charges of violation under the Act. *(Aluminum Tubular Corp., Electrical Workers (IBEW) Local 400 (County of Ocean))*

The NLRB will, under certain circumstances, permit a union to picket a struck employer's trucks while they are on a neutral employer's premises. *(Teamsters Local 279)* But an appeals court found picketing of the entrances to a neutral employer's premises unlawful where the struck employer's trucks were on the premises but out of sight. *(Brown Transport Corp. v. NLRB)*

Another court ruled that the storing of a struck employer's products in an independently owned and operated warehouse did not make the warehouse part of the struck employer's operation for purposes of picketing. Reversing the Board, the court said that the mere presence of the struck employer's goods, under an established business relationship, was not sufficient in itself to convert the unlawful secondary picketing of the warehouse into lawful primary picketing. *(Auburndale Freezer Corp. v. NLRB, Steelworkers v. Auburndale Freezer Corp.)*

Reserved-Gate Picketing

Is the boycott ban violated when a union pickets an industrial plant gate that has been set aside for the exclusive use of neutral contractors and their employees? Such picketing is not unlawful, the Supreme Court has held, if the work being done by the outside contractors using the gate is of a type previously done by the plant's own employees and is more than de minimis in amount. *(Electrical Workers (IUE) Local 761 v. NLRB)*

The Court later held that a union lawfully picketed a gate to a railroad spur track adjacent to a struck plant, even though the gate was on the railroad's property and was used exclusively by railroad employees. The picketing was protected primary activity, the Court said, since it occurred at a situs proximate to and related to the day-to-day operations of the struck plant. *(Steelworkers v. NLRB)*

But the Court's "normal operations" test does not apply to picketing of a reserved gate at a construction project *(New Orleans Building and Construction Trades Council v. NLRB (Markwell & Hartz, Inc.))*; such picketing must meet the common-situs picketing tests. *(NLRB v. Nashville Building and Construction Trades Council)* The normal operations test also cannot be used to justify picketing of a manufacturer's plant in furtherance of a dispute with maintenance contractors working there. *(NLRB v. Plumbers Local 60)* And picketing does not become lawful merely because employees of the struck employer work side-by-side with employees of neutrals and there is a certain amount of communication between them. *(Auto Workers Local 422 v. NLRB)*

Reversing the Board, an appeals court held that a union unlawfully followed the truck of a ready-mix concrete supplier through a reserved gate at a construction site and picketed "between the headlights" while the truck was making a delivery there. The reserved-gate system gave the union a reasonable alternative, the court said. *(Allied Concrete, Inc. v. NLRB)* Another court said that unlawful intent could not be presumed where the neutral reserved gate which the union picketed was effectively hidden from public view. *(Electrical Workers (IBEW) Local 501 v. NLRB (Pond Electric Service))*

In all of these boycott cases, the Board will *not* consider the picketing a violation if the struck company and the picketed company have common ownership and control so that they are regarded as one "employer" under the law or if there is an ally relationship between the two. An ally relationship was found to exist in one case, for example, where the picketed companies "knowingly" were doing struck work and were being paid for doing it directly or indirectly by the struck company. *(NLRB v. Electrical Workers (IUE) Local 459)*

The ally doctrine is discussed at length in the Board's *Curtin Matheson* decision.

HOT-CARGO CONTRACTS

As used by labor unions, the term "hot cargo" refers to goods produced or shipped by an "unfair" employer. In such a context, the term "unfair" may refer to a struck employer, to an employer whose goods bear no union label, or to an employer whose wages or other working conditions are deemed substandard by the union.

As a measure of self-protection, some unions have negotiated contracts giving their members the right to refuse to handle or process hot cargo. Prior to the 1959 amendments to the Act, hot-cargo agreements were not of themselves unlawful. But neither were they a defense to conduct otherwise within the reach of the secondary boycott ban.

The 1959 amendments make it an unfair labor practice for an employer and a union to enter into any agreement under which the employer is to stop handling, selling, transporting, or using the products of any other person or to stop doing business with any other person. Agreements of this type previously entered into are made unenforceable and void.

The broad language used in the ban might encompass not only hot-cargo contracts but also various types of restrictions on subcontracting of work. There are specific exceptions for contracts dealing with jobbing and subcontracting in the clothing industry and job site subcontracting in the construction industry, however.

The hot-cargo ban does not outlaw contracts under which union members may refuse to install prefabricated materials on construction jobs, the Supreme Court has held, since these are work preservation agreements designed to protect work that unit employees regularly and traditionally had performed. *(National Woodwork Manufacturers Association v. NLRB, Houston Insulation Contractors v. NLRB)*

But the Court later held that the hot-cargo prohibition applied to union picketing for an agreement under which a general contractor's job site work would be subcontracted only to firms having labor agreements with the picketing union. The construction industry exception to the hot-cargo ban extends only to agreements in the context of collective bargaining relationships, the Court said, and possibly to common-situs relationships on particular job sites as well. *(Connell Construction Co. v. Plumbers Local 100)* It added, however, that such union-signatory subcontracting clauses are lawful when sought or obtained in the context of a collective bargaining relationship, even if application of the clauses is not limited to particular job sites on which both union and nonunion workers are employed. *(Woelke & Romero Framing v. NLRB)*

The Board misapplied the work preservation doctrine in determining that the rules a longshore union negotiated to govern the loading and unloading of containers in the shipping industry amounted to an unlawful work acquisition agreement, the Supreme Court found. The Board focused on the work done by truckers and consolidators after the introduction of containerized shipping, the Court noted, instead of looking at the work being done by the longshoremen before the introduction of containerization. *(NLRB v. Longshoremen (ILA))* The rules were valid work-preservation agreements, the Court held. *(NLRB v. Longshoremen (ILA) (American Trucking Association))*

RIGHT-TO-CONTROL TEST

After the Supreme Court's decision on refusals to install prefabricated work on construction projects, there remained the issue as to whether the holding applied where the boycotted employer did not have the right to control the use of the prefabricated products on the construction. An example of such noncontrol would be where the specification to use the prefabricated material was made by others, such as the product owner or the general contractor.

The issue was resolved in a case arising out of a union's attempt to enforce a contract providing that the cutting and threading of pipe wold be done at the job site. In finding unlawful the union's refusal to install pipe that had been cut and threaded at the factory, the NLRB properly considered the contracting employer's lack of control over the assignment of such work, the Supreme Court held; this was one of those situations in which courts should defer to the Board's understanding of the statute it administers. (*NLRB v. Plumbers Local 638*)

RIGHTS OF STRIKERS

The Taft-Hartley Act's impact on strikes and picketing is two-sided. It makes certain types of strikes and picketing unlawful but it also extends protection to employees to engage in certain strikes, picketing, and other concerted activities. The degree of protection, if any, depends on what type of strike is involved—economic, unfair labor practice, protected, unprotected, or illegal.

Unfair Labor Practice Strikes

The greatest degree of protection is extended to unfair labor practice strikes. An unfair labor practice strike is one caused or prolonged, in whole or in part, by unfair labor practices of the employer. Participants in such strikes are entitled to reinstatement in their jobs upon unconditional application, even though it may be necessary to discharge replacements to make room for them. Back pay is customarily awarded beginning five days after their unconditional offer to return to work *(Drug Package Co.)*, but unlawfully discharged strikers are entitled to back pay from the time of discharge. *(Abilities & Goodwill, Inc. v. NLRB, NLRB v. Lyon & Ryan Ford, Inc.)*

Strike replacements who were promised permanent jobs but who must be let go to make room for returning unfair labor practice strikers may be able to bring a state-court action against the employer for breach of contract and misrepresentation. *(Belknap, Inc. v. Hale)*

Economic Strikes

The term "economic strike" has been used by the NLRB as a designation for any strike not caused or prolonged by unfair labor practices of the employer. The implication is that it is a strike to enforce economic demands. But the term also embraces a strike for recognition or organization. Economic strikers have only limited reinstatement rights. They may claim their former jobs if permanent replacements have not been hired. But prior to the strikers' application for reinstatement, the employer may protect his business by hiring replacements or by discontinuing jobs for business reasons. If permanent replacements are hired before the strikers apply for reinstatement, the employer may reject the strikers' applications without violating the law. *(NLRB v. Mackay Radio & Telegraph Co.)*

But replaced economic strikers have been ordered reinstated where this was "crucial" to the effectiveness of a bargaining order that had been issued against the employer. The strikers were not awarded back pay. *(Drug Package Co.; see Willenbrink v. NLRB)*

If an economic striker applies for a job as a new employee after the strike is over, the employer may not discriminate against him because of his participation in the strike. This would be an unfair labor practice. Moreover, the Supreme Court has held that an employer may not assure strike replacements some form of job tenure by granting them superseniority at the expense of the strikers. Such action is so inherently discriminatory and destructive of union activity, the Court said, as to violate the Act without regard to the employer's motivation. *(NLRB v. Erie Resistor Corp.)*

Economic strikers remain employees under the Act even after they have been replaced. So they are entitled to reinstatement as vacancies occur in their former jobs unless (1) they have obtained regular and substantially equivalent employment elsewhere in the meantime, or (2) the employer is able to establish legitimate and substantial business reasons to justify his failure to offer reinstatement. *(NLRB v. Fleetwood Trailer Co., Laidlaw Corp. v. NLRB)*

But permanent replacements and reinstated economic strikers may be given recall preference over unreinstated strikers in the event of a layoff, according to one appeals court *(Giddings & Lewis v. NLRB)*, and under certain circumstances, they may be required to notify the company at six-month intervals of their continued interest in reinstatement. *(Giddings & Lewis v. NLRB)* When an employer is charged with unlawfully recalling laid-off permanent strike replacements ahead of unreinstated strikers, the NLRB's approach is to require its General Counsel to establish a prima facie case that the layoff of the replacements truly signified their "departure" and thus created vacancies that the unreinstated strikers were entitled to fill. The employer must then show that no such vacancy occurred or that its failure to recall the strikers was based on legitimate and substantial business justifications. *(Aqua-Chem, Inc.)*

Food Stamp Act

An amendment to the Food Stamp Act providing that no household shall become eligible to participate in the food stamp program while any member of the household is on strike is valid under the First and Fifth Amendments to the U.S. Constitution, the Supreme Court has ruled. *(Lyng v. Auto Workers)*

Unprotected Strikes

Participants in unprotected strikes are not protected against discharge by their employer. Included in such strikes are not only those that are unlawful but also some not specifically forbidden by law. The penalty for an unprotected strike falls directly on the strikers, since they lose their reinstatement rights.

Unprotected strikes under the rulings of the courts and the Board include the following:

- Strikes that violate federal laws other than the Taft-Hartley Act, such as the laws against mutiny. *(Southern Steamship Co. v. NLRB)*
- Sit-down strikes. *(NLRB v. Fansteel Metallurgical Corp.)*
- Strikes in violation of collective bargaining contracts. *(NLRB v. Sands Manufacturing Co.)*
- Slowdowns and partial strikes, such as a refusal to work overtime. *(NLRB v. Montgomery Ward & Co., Elk Lumber Co.)*
- Wildcat strikes in derogation of the bargaining agent's authority, as when a minority group of employees strikes to affect the course of negotiations without the union's authorization. *(NLRB v. Draper Corp.)*
- A strike by a group of white employees to force their employer to fire all black employees. *(NLRB General Counsel Administrative Ruling, Case No. 56)*
- A walkout during working hours for the purpose of attending a union meeting. *(NLRB General Counsel Administrative Ruling, Case No. 778)*
- A strike for political reasons, such as a strike to put pressure on a state legislature to pass a bill supported by the union. *(NLRB v. Bretz Fuel Co.)*
- A strike to protest a foreman's demotion. The walkout was said to be in the interest of the foreman, rather than the employees. *(NLRB v. Reynolds International Pen Co.)*
- "Hit-and-run" or intermittent strikes. *(Pacific Telephone Co.)*
- A strike in which a picket called customers crossing the picket line obscene names. The offending picket lost her protection under the Act. *(Montgomery Ward & Co. v. NLRB)*

During the period of World War II wage and price controls, the NLRB held that employees who struck to compel their employer to give them a wage increase in excess of that allowed under the stabilization program lost their protection under the Act. So the employer was held not to have committed an unfair labor practice under the Act by discharging the strikers. *(American News Co., Inc.)*

Strike During Cooling-Off Period

In an effort to encourage the resolution of contract disputes through bargaining, the Taft-Hartley Act lays down some strict procedures that must be followed before a party to a contract may engage in a strike or lockout over an attempt to modify or terminate a contract.

Before modifying or terminating a contract, a party must take these steps:

- A written notice must be served on the other party 60 days prior to the contract's expiration date or, if there is no expiration date, 60 days prior to the date on which it is proposed to modify or terminate the contract.
- An offer must be made to confer with the other party to negotiate the desired changes.
- The party must notify the Federal Mediation and Conciliation Service and any mediation agency within the state if the dispute still exists 30 days after the original notice was given to the other party.
- The moving party must permit the contract to continue in full force and effect, without resorting to strike or lockout, for 60 days after the original notice was given or until the expiration date of the contract, whichever occurs later.

Employees who strike during the 60-day cooling-off period forfeit their status as "employees" under the Act and are not protected against being discharged or otherwise disciplined by the employer for participating in the strike. This loss of protection, however, does not apply to a strike not involving "contract termination or modification." It has been held, for example, that the 60-day notice and cooling-off period does not apply to a strike caused by serious unfair labor practices of the employer not involving contract issues. *(Mastro Plastics Corp. v. NLRB)*

The burden of giving the statutory notice to mediation services rests exclusively with the party wishing to modify or terminate the contract. *(United Artists)*

STRIKES IN VIOLATION OF NO-STRIKE CLAUSES

The Norris-LaGuardia Act does not bar injunctive relief against a strike called by a union in violation of a no-strike clause in a collective bargaining contract, the Supreme Court held, where (1) the grievance leading to the strike was subject to arbitration under the contract, (2) the employer was ready to proceed with arbitration, and (3) the employer suffered irreparable injury from the breach of the no-strike obligation. *(Boys Markets, Inc. v. Retail Clerks)*

But the Court later held that a union could not be enjoined from engaging in a "sympathy" strike—a refusal to cross a sister local's picket lines—pending an arbitrator's decision on whether the sympathy strike was forbidden under the no-strike clause of the union's labor agreement. The sympathy strike was not over any dispute between the union and the employer that was even remotely subject to the arbitration provisions of the contract, the Court said. *(Buffalo Forge Co. v. Steelworkers)*

The Court relied on this ruling in holding that a union's politically motivated refusal to load Soviet-bound cargo on ships was a "labor dispute" covered by the Norris-LaGuardia Act and therefore could not be enjoined pending arbitration of the legality of the work stoppage. *(Jacksonville Bulk Terminals v. Longshoremen (ILA))*

In the NLRB's view, a broad no-strike clause is a clear and unmistakable waiver of the right to engage in sympathy strikes or honor stranger picket lines—unless the contract or extrinsic evidence shows that the clause was not intended to cover sympathy strikes. In deciding whether sympathy strikes fall within the scope of a no-strike provision, the parties' actual intent is to be given controlling weight and extrinsic evidence should be considered as an integral part of the analysis. *(Indianapolis Power & Light Co.)* Appeals courts have basically agreed with the Board's approach. *(Electrical Workers (IBEW) Local 803 v. NLRB, Electrical Workers (IBEW) Local 1395 v. NLRB)*

A waiver of the right to engage in sympathy strikes was found where the no-strike clause was functionally independent of the arbitration clause and derived from the parties' common interest in avoiding interruptions of plant operations. *(United States Steel Corp. v. NLRB)*

Unless an employer obtains a contractual waiver that is clear and unmistakable, union officials who take part in a wildcat strike may not be disciplined more severely than rank-and-file employee participants. *(Metropolitan Edison Co. v. NLRB)* But a contract that required the union to "exert itself to bring about a quick termination" of wildcat strikes was found to be a clear and unmistakable waiver of union stewards' statutory protection from disparate discipline. *(Indiana & Michigan Electric Co.)* And union officials who lead unlawful strikes may be disciplined more severely than rank-and-file employees who engage in similar conduct. *(Midwest Precision Castings Co.)*

The Supreme Court has upheld the jurisdiction of a state court to enjoin a work stoppage called in violation of a no-strike clause in a contract providing a binding-settlement procedure, even though the strike arguably was an unfair labor practice under the Act's forced-work-assignment provisions. *(Arnold Co. v. Carpenters District Council)*

NATIONAL EMERGENCY STRIKES

There is another class of strikes that, although not unlawful in themselves, may be delayed or postponed under the Act. These are the so-called national emergency strikes—those that affect an entire or substantial part of an industry and that, if permitted to occur, would in the opinion of the President imperil the national health or safety.

Such strikes may be postponed up to 80 days under a procedure entailing these steps: (1) appointment of a board of inquiry to report to the President the facts of the dispute, but without recommendations; (2) petition to a federal court for an injunction restraining the strike; (3) resumption of bargaining by the parties; (4) reconvening of the board of inquiry to report, 60 days after the issuance of an injunction, on the state of the negotiations and the employer's last offer; (5) publication of the report; (6) polling of the employees by the NLRB within the next 15 days as to acceptance of the employer's last offer; (7) petition for dissolution of the injunction at the close of 80 days; and (8) a report by the President to Congress, with recommendations.

A challenge to the constitutionality of these provisions and to an injunction issued under them in the 1959 basic steel strike was rejected by the Supreme Court. *(Steelworkers v. United States)*

The Railway Labor Act also contains procedures for dealing with national emergency strikes, but it has been necessary for Congress to adopt *ad hoc* legislation requiring compulsory arbitration of disputes in the railroad industry. There have been many proposals in Congress to revise completely the rules dealing with national emergency strikes.

THE RULES GOVERNING LOCKOUTS

A lockout is the term applied to an employer's action in temporarily closing his plant and laying off the workers during a labor dispute. It is often looked upon as the employer's counterpart of the union's strike weapon. And, like the strike, it is subject to some restrictions under the Taft-Hartley Act.

Under Section 7 of the Act, employees are guaranteed the right to engage in "concerted activities" for their mutual aid or protection. So an employer violates the Act when he locks out his employees for the purpose of defeating their organizational efforts or of impeding or discouraging other protected concerted activities. *(NLRB v. Somerset Classics, Inc., NLRB v. Wallick & Schwalm Co.)*

For some years, whether the NLRB found other types of lockouts lawful or unlawful was likely to depend on whether the lockout was "offensive" or "defensive." The employer could not use an offensive lockout as the counterpart to the union's strike weapon, it said, but an employer could use a defensive lockout in unusual economic circumstances—such as where a threatened strike at a bottling company would have resulted in a costly spoilage of syrup. *(Duluth Bottling Association)*

But in 1965, the Supreme Court found no Taft-Hartley violation where an employer, after impasse had been reached in contract negotiations, shut down his plant and laid off his employees temporarily for the purpose of bringing economic pressure to bear in support of his legitimate bargaining position. The Court left open the question whether the employer could have hired replacements—temporary or permanent—and continued operations. *(American Ship Building Co. v. NLRB)*

Employers have been permitted to resort to preimpasse lockouts in some situations. *(Darling & Co., Lane v. NLRB)*

The Board has held that an employer's hiring of permanent replacements during a lockout violated the Act. *(Johns-Manville Products Corp. v. NLRB)*

The Board currently holds, with court approval, that an employer may use temporary replacements to carry on operations during any otherwise lawful lockout, including a lockout initiated solely to bring economic pressure to bear in support of a legitimate economic position, absent specific proof of anti-union motivation. *(Harter Equipment, Operating Engineers Local 825 v. NLRB)*

The Board abandoned its earlier position, approved by another appeals court, that the use of temporary replacements during an offensive lockout was unlawful. *(Inland Trucking Co. v. NLRB)*

An employer may lawfully continue operations during an offensive lockout by using its own supervisors and other non-union personnel, without hiring outside replacements. *(Ottawa Silica Co. v. NLRB)*

Where a union "whipsaws" a multiemployer bargaining group by striking one member, the Supreme Court permitted the other members to lock out their employees as a means of preserving the integrity of the bargaining unit. *(NLRB v. Truck Drivers Local 449)* It also has permitted them to continue operations by hiring temporary replacements for the locked-out employees. *(NLRB v. Brown)*

CROSSING PICKET LINE

An employee has a right to honor a lawful picket line set up by his union at his plant, although if the strike is for economic reasons he may be permanently replaced, as discussed above. If the picket line is set up by another union representing other employees at the plant, the NLRB's position is that the employee has the right to refuse to cross the picket line and may not be disciplined or discharged for this reason; but he may be treated as an economic striker subject to replacement. *(Newbery Energy Corp.)* Federal appeals courts, however, are in disagreement as to the right of an employee to refuse to cross such a picket line. *(NLRB v. Illinois Bell Telephone Co., NLRB v. Southern Greyhound Lines)*

Employees who refuse to cross a picket line established by unfair labor practice strikers are themselves unfair labor practice strikers and therefore cannot be permanently replaced, the Board has held. *(C. K. Smith & Co., Inc.)* But employees who refuse to cross a picket line may be disciplined, the Board has found, if the picket line in fact was established in violation of the contract. *(American Telephone & Telegraph Co.)*

Where there is a lawful, authorized picket line at the plant of another employer, a proviso to the Act protects an employee against reprisal or discharge for refusing to cross the picket line, and the proviso has been held to validate contracts expressly permitting employees to decline to cross such picket lines in the course of their duties. But an employee loses that protection if there is a no-strike clause in the contract.

Where no contract provision applies, one way or the other, and employees such as pickup-and-delivery workers refuse to cross picket lines at the premises of other employers, the federal appeals courts are in disagreement as to whether the refusal is protected. *(NLRB v. William S. Carroll, Inc.)* The NLRB's view is that the refusal is protected, but that the employees may be discharged if this is necessary for the efficient operation of their employer's business. *(Teamsters Local 79 v. NLRB)*

Union Fines

A union may fine members for crossing a lawful picket line set up by the union and may sue to collect the fines, the U.S. Supreme Court has held. *(NLRB v. Allis-Chalmers Manufacturing Co.)* But such fines are unlawful where employees resign their union membership before crossing the picket line. *(Machinists*

Lodge 405 v. NLRB) State courts, not the NLRB, have the authority to determine whether such fines are "reasonable" in amount. *(Auto Workers Local 248 v. Natzke, NLRB v. Boeing Co.)*
See Chapter 9 for a further discussion of this issue.

RACIAL DISCRIMINATION PICKETING

Generally, employees are engaged in unprotected activity when they bypass their union and its contractual grievance procedure and resort to walkouts and picketing to bring direct pressure on their employer to comply with their demands.

The Supreme Court has refused to make an exception to this principle for protests against employment practices that allegedly discriminate on racial grounds. It upheld the discharge of two black employees who picketed their employer's store and urged a consumer boycott in support of their claim that the employer had racially discriminatory employment practices, where their union was trying to resolve the discrimination issue through the contractual grievance procedure. *(Emporium Capwell Co. v. Western Addition Community Organization)*

PICKETING AS FREE SPEECH

In the 1968 *Logan Valley Plaza* case, the Supreme Court held that the First Amendment barred a state court from enjoining union picketing in the parcel-pickup zone and parking lot of a shopping center.

But in the 1972 *Central Hardware* case, involving solicitation by union organizers in retail store parking lots, the Court said the *Logan Valley Plaza* holding was limited to shopping centers of such public scale that they in effect acquire the characteristics of a public municipal facility. The case before it was not a constitutional law case but a Taft-Hartley case, the Court found.

The Court therefore concluded that the applicable principles were those laid down in the *Babcock & Wilcox* case, to the effect that an employer may bar nonemployee solicitation on his property where (1) the union may reach employees by making reasonable efforts through other available channels, and (2) the no-solicitation order does not discriminate against the union by allowing other solicitation or distribution.

In 1976, the Court announced that *Logan Valley Plaza* had been overruled. Employees have no First Amendment right to picket a retail store in a privately owned shopping mall, it said; the rights of the parties in such situations depend exclusively on the Taft-Hartley Act. *(Hudgens v. NLRB)*

NLRB Approach

In accommodating an individual's exercise of rights under the Taft-Hartley Act with a property owner's right against intrusions by those whom he has not invited to enter, the Board balances the degree of impairment of statutory rights if access is denied against the degree of impairment of the property right if access is granted. The Board now holds that the availability of reasonably effective alternative means of communication is a factor that must be considered in every case. *(Jean Country)* The Board had previously held that alternative means would only be considered when the strengths of the statutory and property rights were relatively equal. *(Fairmont Hotel)*

Trespass

An action to enjoin union picketing that allegedly violated a state trespass law could be maintained even though the picketing was both arguably protected and arguably prohibited by the Taft-Hartley Act, the Supreme Court held. The issue before the state court was not identical to the one that could have been presented to the NLRB, the Court said, and the union could have gone to the Board but failed to do so even after the employer demanded that the union's pickets be removed from his property. *(Sears, Roebuck & Co. v. San Diego County District Council of Carpenters)*

EXTORTIONATE PICKETING

The 1959 Landrum-Griffin Act makes it a federal crime for a union or individual to engage in "extortionate" picketing. This is defined as picketing for the personal profit or enrichment of any individual, except through a bona fide increase in wages or other employee benefits, by taking or obtaining any money or other thing of value from the employer against his will or with his consent.

8
SETTLEMENT OF DISPUTES

A measure of the successful conduct of labor relations is the degree in which disputes between management and employees are promptly and satisfactorily settled. Basically, there are two types of disputes. First, there are those involving conflicting management and union interests—those that are settled by the execution of a collective bargaining agreement. Second, there are disputes relating to rights under the contract. These usually are settled under the grievance procedure and, if that fails, by arbitration.

There are other types of disputes that affect labor relations. There are, for example, disputes between labor unions. These may be settled in a number of ways—by an impartial umpire or a joint board set up by the unions themselves, by the NLRB, or by the courts.

ROLE OF THE MEDIATION SERVICE

To provide assistance to management and labor in settling contract disputes, the Taft-Hartley Act set up the Federal Mediation and Conciliation Service. The duties of the Service in seeking to settle a dispute are outlined in the law as first conciliation, then mediation, and finally an effort to obtain consent for a vote by the employees on the employer's last offer. Conciliation is distinguished from mediation in that conciliation is the effort to get parties to agree to offers freely made by either side, while mediation entails suggestions by the third party of bases for settlement that had not been put forward by either side.

In addition to giving the FMCS these functions, the law requires that the Service be notified of all disputes over renewal or modification of contracts if no settlement has been reached 30 days after a desire for a change has been indicated. State mediation agencies must be notified at the same time. The Federal Service screens out cases that do not affect interstate commerce and those that affect it to a minor degree, leaving these to the state agencies to handle.

The FMCS also maintains a roster of arbitrators for referral to unions and employers. This will be discussed in more detail later.

Hospital Disputes

In 1974, Congress passed a law extending the coverage of the Taft-Hartley Act to private nonprofit hospitals and nursing homes. The NLRB previously had asserted jurisdiction over proprietary hospitals and nursing homes. *(Butte Medical Properties, University Nursing Home, Inc.)*

The provisions of the Act and the new procedures apply equally to all proprietary and private nonprofit hospitals, convalescent hospitals, health maintenance organizations, health or medical clinics, nursing homes, extended care facilities, and other institutions devoted to the care of sick, infirm, or aged persons. A medical school affiliated with a hospital may be a health care institution. *(Kirksville College)*

The dispute settlement procedures under the law are as follows:

- Ninety days before contract termination, the party seeking termination must notify the other party in writing.
- Sixty days before termination, the initiating party must notify the FMCS that the existing contract will expire. On receiving the 60-day notice, the FMCS is to contact the parties in an effort to achieve a settlement. The parties are required to participate in meetings called by the FMCS.

- Thirty days before termination, the Director of the FMCS may invoke a 30-day "cooling off" period, during which there is to be no strike or lockout, and convene a board of inquiry to look into the dispute.
- Fifteen days before termination, the board makes its findings of fact and recommendations for settlement.

Initial Bargaining

There is a different time schedule where the parties are bargaining for their first contract. The FMCS would receive only a 30-day notice of an existing dispute and its potential threat to health care delivery. The Service then would have only 10 days to opt to invoke the board-of-inquiry procedure. Again, if a board were appointed, it would have 15 days in which to compile the facts and issue recommendations for settlement, which would be made public.

Notice of Strike

Failure of the FMCS to settle a dispute relating to either an initial or a renewal contract within the required notice periods does not necessarily leave the union free to resort to self-help at once. Section 8(g) requires that the union give the employer a 10-day notice of its intent to strike or picket. The delay is to enable the employer to make plans for the continuity of patient care.

In the case of disputes relating to an initial contract, the 10-day notice may not be served until the 30-day notice period has elapsed. So a union seeking an initial contract may not engage in strikes or picketing until 40 days following its notice to the FMCS that a dispute exists.

Appeals courts have held that the 10-day notice requirement applies only where a union represents or seeks to represent health care employees. (*NLRB v. Electrical Workers (IBEW) Local 388, Laborers Local 1057 v. NLRB*) The NLRB does not agree. (*Painters Local 452*)

A union may unilaterally decide to start its strike or picketing at a time later than was set forth in the 10-day notice, the

NLRB has held, but any unilateral extension beyond 72 hours is unreasonable, and even within the 72-hour period, the union should give at least 12 hours' notice of the actual time when picketing is to begin. *(Retail, Wholesale & Department Store Employees District 1199-E)*

The 10-day notice requirement does not apply to mere threats to strike, the NLRB has ruled. *(Retail, Wholesale & Department Store Employees District 1199-E)*

ARBITRATION OF DISPUTES

Just as commercial arbitration arose as a less expensive alternative to litigation, so labor arbitration has served as a less expensive alternative to a strike. It also may be resorted to as an alternative to a suit for breach of a collective bargaining contract.

When an employer and a union agree to arbitrate a dispute, each is giving up a right otherwise enjoyed. For example:

- *For the employer*, it means that he is giving up his right to take unilateral action on the matter under dispute.
- *For the union*, it means that it is giving up the right to strike over the issue submitted.
- *And for both*, it means that failure to abide by the decision of the neutral party empowered to decide the dispute could lead to a suit for enforcement of the award.

Arbitration proceedings usually begin with a submission agreement and the selection of an arbitrator. The submission agreement confers authority upon the arbitrator and defines the extent of that authority. If carefully drawn, the submission will state (1) the nature of the grievance, (2) the claim of the aggrieved party, (3) reference to the specific contract clause relied upon, (4) the relief sought, and (5) the retroactive or effective date of application of any award.

In some cases, the selection of an arbitrator is no problem. The contract between the employer and the union will designate a permanent umpire or arbitrator to handle all disputes arising under the contract. But under the majority of contracts, a temporary or *ad hoc* arbitrator must be selected for each dispute referred to arbitration.

Where a temporary arbitrator is to be used, the contracts usually specify alternative methods of selection. If the parties are unable to agree on an arbitrator within a specified period of time, the contract provides for designation of an arbitrator by an impartial agency. Most contracts designate either the Federal Mediation and Conciliation Service or the American Arbitration Association as the selecting agency.

Under the rules of the American Arbitration Association, the parties may make their own selection from lists provided by the Association. The parties may cross off names they object to, and the Association will choose from those remaining in order of preference. If no agreement can be reached on names on the lists, the Association will appoint an arbitrator not on the lists.

The Federal Mediation and Conciliation Service also maintains a roster of experienced and qualified arbitrators from which the parties to a labor agreement may make their selection. Here again, the parties may select an arbitrator by striking those to whom they object from the list or by advising the FMCS of the order of preference among those on the panel.

ARBITRATION PROCEDURE

In a typical arbitration proceeding, the arbitrator communicates with the parties to arrange a hearing date. The parties may stipulate use of a specific hearing procedure, such as that suggested by the American Arbitration Association. Usually, however, the hearing procedure is determined by the arbitrator.

The formality of the hearing before the arbitrator will depend, in part, on the nature of the issues, the character of the parties, and the circumstances of the dispute. Formal hearings resembling legal trials sometimes are used, but most hearings are as informal as the orderly presentation of the evidence will allow.

In any case, all parties must be given an opportunity to be heard, which implies the right to receive notice of the hearing. If rights of a third party are involved, he should be given notice and opportunity to attend the hearing. The arbitrator has the responsibility of giving notice. The parties must be allowed to present evidence without unreasonable restriction and must be allowed to cross-examine adverse witnesses.

Arbitrators generally have wide discretion as to the observance of the rules of evidence. But an arbitrator may not apply technical evidentiary principles to exclude material and pertinent evidence unless he has announced at the outset of the hearing that the rules of evidence are to be adhered to strictly. *(Harvey Aluminum, Inc. v. Steelworkers)*

Neither the arbitrator nor the witnesses need be sworn unless required by a statute in the state. A majority of the states have some type of provision for the swearing of witnesses but not all make it compulsory upon the parties. The parties may make oral argument at the conclusion of the evidence, but they may waive the right. If the parties desire to file written briefs or if the arbitrator feels that it is desirable, briefs will be filed. The parties decide whether to have a written record of the hearing.

At the conclusion of the proceeding, the arbitrator renders an award that, by prior agreement of the parties, is final and binding.

NLRB's DEFERRAL TO ARBITRATION

In the 1955 *Spielberg* case, the NLRB decided it would honor an arbitration award involving the same issue raised in a charge filed with the Board where (1) the arbitration proceedings appeared to have been "fair and regular," (2) all parties had agreed to be bound by the award, and (3) the arbitration decision was not clearly repugnant to the purposes and policies of the Act. The Board later added that the arbitrator must have considered the issue in the charge filed with the Board. *(Spielberg Manufacturing Co.)*

The party arguing against deferral must establish the existence of deficiencies in the arbitration process requiring that the award be ignored. Deferral may be warranted if the contractual issue is factually parallel to the unfair labor practice issue, the arbitrator was presented generally with the facts relevant to the unfair labor practice issue, and his award—though not necessarily totally consistent with NLRB precedent—is susceptible of an interpretation consistent with the Taft-Hartley Act. *(Olin Corp.)*

One appeals court ruled that the Board's *Olin* standard does not sufficiently protect employees' rights granted by the Taft-Hartley Act. By presuming, until proven otherwise, that all arbitration proceedings confront and decide every possible unfair labor practice issue, the *Olin* standard gives away too much of the Board's responsibility. *(Taylor v. NLRB)*

The *Spielberg* doctrine will not be applied where it is alleged that an employee was discharged or disciplined for invoking or participating in the processes of the NLRB. *(Filmation Associates)*

The principle of honoring arbitration awards that meet the specified standards was extended to representation cases in the 1963 *Raley's, Inc.* decision.

Collyer Doctrine

If a collective bargaining contract contains a grievance-arbitration procedure for resolving disputes under the contract, the NLRB will defer to the contractual procedure where an unfair labor practice charge also involving a contractual issue has been filed with the Board prior to arbitration. But the Board will retain jurisdiction over the dispute for the purpose of entertaining an appropriate and timely motion for further consideration upon a proper showing that either (1) the dispute has not been resolved either by amicable settlement in the grievance procedure with reasonable promptness after the Board's deferral decision or submitted promptly to arbitration or (2) the grievance or arbitration procedures have not been fair and regular or have reached a result that is repugnant to the Act. *(Collyer Insulated Wire)*

The *Collyer* case involved an alleged violation by the employer of his bargaining duty by taking unilateral action on a matter subject to bargaining. The *Collyer* doctrine later was expanded to discharge and other types of cases; it is not limited to unfair labor practice allegations involving breach of the duty to bargain. *(United Technologies)*

The *Collyer* ruling will not be applied where both the employer and the union are "hostile" to the interests of the employees involved. *(Kansas Meat Packers)*

The deferral-to-arbitration principles established in *Spielberg* and *Collyer* also apply to settlements reached under contractual grievance procedures without going to arbitration. *(Alpha Beta Co.)*

ARBITRATION AND CIVIL RIGHTS ACTS, FLSA

In a unanimous opinion, the Supreme Court held in 1974 that a discharged employee whose claim of racial discrimination was rejected by an arbitrator was not barred by the doctrine of waiver nor the federal labor policy favoring arbitration from bringing an action on the same claim under Title VII of the Civil Rights Act of 1964. Moreover, the federal courts are not required to defer to the arbitrator's decision but, instead, should provide a trial *de novo* on the employee's claim. *(Alexander v. Gardner-Denver Co.)*

The Court, however, pointed out that when an arbitration decision gives full consideration to Title VII rights, a court may give such a decision "great weight," particularly where the issue is solely one of fact and based on an adequate record.

An arbitrator's back-pay award in favor of employees laid off in violation of contractual seniority provisions was entitled to judicial enforcement, the Supreme Court held, even though the layoffs were pursuant to a conciliation agreement that the employer and the EEOC had signed and that conflicted with the employer's collective bargaining contract. The Court noted that the arbitration award did not require the employer to violate the conciliation agreement, but simply held the employer liable for its breach of contract. *(W. R. Grace & Co. v. Rubber Workers Local 759)*

The filing of a grievance does not toll the limitations period for filing a charge with the Equal Employment Opportunity Commission, the Supreme Court later held. *(Electrical Workers (IUE) Local 790 v. Robbins & Myers, Inc.)*

Neither the acceptance of an arbitration award by a charging party nor his filing or settlement of a Title VII action precludes the EEOC from suing the employer in the public interest, a federal appeals court has ruled. *(EEOC v. McLean Trucking Co.)*

But one appeals court held binding in a subsequent Title VII action an arbitrator's findings that a black laid-off employee was not entitled to retroactive seniority under a collective bargaining contract and that past practice was not controlling. The court said that the arbitral decision is final and binding to the extent that it resolves questions of contractual rights. (*Owens v. Texaco, Inc.*)

An arbitrator's determination that an employer had just cause to discharge a black employee did not preclude the employee from suing under the Civil Rights Act of 1866. (*Wilmington v. J.I. Case Co.*)

FLSA

Arbitration awards upholding an employer's failure to pay over-the-road drivers for time spent in pretrip inspections of their trucks did not bar the drivers' portal-to-portal claims under the Fair Labor Standards Act, the U.S. Supreme Court held. (*Barrentine v. Arkansas-Best Freight System*)

In other cases arising under the FLSA, it has been held that employees are not required to exhaust grievance-arbitration machinery before suing for statutory overtime pay (*Iowa Beef Packers, Inc. v. Thompson*) or for pay for participating in a walk-around OSHA inspection during regular working hours. (*Leone v. Mobil Oil Corp.*)

ARBITRATION OF NEW CONTRACTS

The arbitration of new-contract terms or "interest" arbitration has seen only limited use in the private sector of the economy—as, for example, in the Experimental Negotiating Agreement between the Steelworkers and the basic steel companies, under which issues not resolved by negotiations were to be submitted to arbitration. An interest-arbitration provision is not a mandatory subject for bargaining on which an employer or union can insist to the point of impasse during negotiations for a collective bargaining contract. (*NLRB v. Columbus Printing Pressmen Local 252*)

The public sector, in contrast, has used "interest" arbitration to a considerable extent. There also has been resort to fact-finding, with or without recommendations; final-offer arbitration, under which both parties submit final offers to a board of neutrals, which selects one as the final settlement; and "med-arb," under which the person selected by the parties tries first to resolve the dispute by mediation and then, if that fails, issues a binding arbitration award. State statutes providing for interest arbitration in the health care industry have been preempted by the Taft-Hartley Act. *(NLRB v. Massachusetts Nurses Association)*

ENFORCEMENT OF ARBITRATION

At common law, an agreement to arbitrate, while not illegal, was revocable any time before rendition of the award and could not be specifically enforced in the courts. But this has been changed by Section 301 of the Taft-Hartley Act, which gives the federal district courts jurisdiction of suits for breaches of collective bargaining contracts.

In 1957, the U.S. Supreme Court ruled that Section 301 gives the federal courts jurisdiction to order the performance of employer-union contracts to arbitrate disputes. *(Textile Workers v. Lincoln Mills)*

As a follow-up to this decision, the Supreme Court since has laid down some rules to guide the federal courts in enforcing both arbitration agreements and arbitration awards. In brief, the rules are as follows:

- Unless the contract specifies otherwise, an employee must attempt to use the grievance-arbitration procedure of the union contract in pressing a grievance before resorting to the courts. *(Republic Steel Corp. v. NLRB)*
- The question of the arbitrability of a dispute is for the courts to decide, unless the parties clearly state to the contrary. *(Steelworkers v. Warrior & Gulf Navigation Co., AT&T Technologies, Inc. v. Communications Workers of America)*
- This, however, does not give the courts authority to decide questions of contract interpretation or application.

The parties agreed to let arbitrators pass on the merits of a dispute because they believed arbitrators are better equipped to perform this task than are the courts; the parties' wishes should be respected. Moreover, questions of "procedural arbitrability," such as whether the grievance procedure has been complied with, are so intertwined with the merits that they also are for the arbitrator to decide. *(Steelworkers v. Warrior & Gulf Navigation Co., John Wiley & Sons v. Livingston)*

- When a party seeks enforcement of an arbitration clause, the court's only job is to determine whether the contract contains a promise to arbitrate the dispute. A court may not refuse to order arbitration merely because it considers a grievance baseless. *(Steelworkers v. American Manufacturing Co.)*
- A court may not modify or refuse to enforce an arbitration award merely because it disagrees with the arbitrator's interpretation of the contract. If the parties agree to make arbitration final and binding, the courts should not substitute their judgment for that of the arbitrator. *(Steelworkers v. Enterprise Wheel & Car Corp.)*
- Although state courts have concurrent jurisdiction with the federal courts over actions brought under Section 301 of the Taft-Hartley Act to enforce collective bargaining contracts, the state courts must apply federal law wherever there is a conflict. *(Charles Dowd Box Co. v. Courtney, Teamsters Local 174 v. Lucas Flour Co.)*
- If a union has agreed to submit a certain type of dispute to final and binding arbitration, it violates the contract if it strikes over such a dispute. It is not necessary that the contract contain an express no-strike pledge. *(Teamsters Local 174 v. Lucas Flour Co., Gateway Coal Co. v. Mine Workers)*
- But a work stoppage in violation of a collective bargaining contract does not necessarily give the employer the right to refuse to arbitrate the grievance that caused the stoppage of work. The operation of the grievance-arbitration provisions of the contract is not dependent upon the union's observance of the no-strike clause. The employer

may sue for damages in a federal district court. *(Packinghouse Workers Local 721 v. Needham Packing Co.)*

- Moreover, if a union strikes in violation of a no-strike clause in a collective bargaining contract, a federal district court has jurisdiction to issue an order enjoining the strike where (1) the grievance leading to the strike is subject to arbitration under the contract, (2) the employer is ready to proceed with arbitration, and (3) the employer suffered irreparable injury from the union's breach of its no-strike obligation. *(Boys Markets, Inc. v. Retail Clerks)*

- But a union could not be enjoined from engaging in a "sympathy" strike—a refusal to cross a sister local's picket lines—pending an arbitrator's decision on whether the sympathy strike was forbidden under the no-strike clause of the union's labor agreement. The sympathy strike was not over any dispute between the union and the employer that was even remotely subject to the arbitration provisions of the contract. *(Buffalo Forge Co. v. Steelworkers)*

- A damage action brought by an employer for a union's alleged breach of a no-strike contract may not be dismissed or stayed pending arbitration where the contract limits arbitration to employee grievances. But such an action should be stayed pending arbitration where the arbitration clause in the contract is sufficiently broad to cover the claim. *(Atkinson v. Sinclair Refining Co., Drake Bakeries v. Bakery Workers)*

- The courts may enforce arbitration in suits brought under Section 301 even though the conduct involved also may be an unfair labor practice within the NLRB's jurisdiction. *(Carey v. Westinghouse Electric Corp.)*

- The arbitration provision of a union contract may survive the disappearance of the employer by merger so as to be binding on a successor employer. *(John Wiley & Sons v. Livingston; but see Howard Johnson Co. v. Detroit Joint Board)*

- A union's claim for severance pay under an expired collective bargaining contract was arbitrable; "where the dispute is over a provision of the expired agreement, the presumptions favoring arbitrability must be negated expressly or by clear implication." *(Nolde Brothers v. Bakery Workers)*

- A dispute concerning a mine operator's continued employment of foremen who failed to carry out certain prescribed safety procedures was arbitrable under an arbitration provision covering "any local trouble of any kind arising at the mine." *(Gateway Coal Co. v. Mine Workers)*

- A court may refuse to enforce an arbitrator's interpretation of a contract only when the contract as interpreted would violate a well-defined and explicit public policy, not a formulation of public policy based only on general considerations of supposed public interests. However, a public policy based on "general considerations of supposed public interests" is not a ground to invalidate an arbitration award rendered in accord with a valid labor contract. *(W. R. Grace & Co. v. Rubber Workers Local 759, Paperworkers v. Misco, Inc.)*

- An employee who seeks to have an arbitrator invalidate disciplinary action by a federal agency must show that the agency committed harmful error that resulted in substantial prejudice to the employee's individual rights. A contract violation that harms only the union is not enough. *(Cornelius v. Nutt)*

Other Rulings

Rulings of federal appeals courts in cases involving the enforcement of arbitration agreements and arbitration awards include the following:

- Two arbitration cases involving the competing work claims of two unions could be consolidated, where each union's contract contained a broad arbitration clause. One union demanded arbitration under its contract with the employer, and the employer demanded arbitration under his contract with the second union. *(CBS v. American Recording & Broadcasting Association)*

- An award issued by a union-appointed arbitrator acting alone was not entitled to enforcement even though the collective bargaining contract permitted the arbitrator appointed by one party to arbitrate a grievance under certain conditions if the other party failed to appoint its representative. The clause permitting single-party arbitration applied only where a party named no representative whatever to the board of arbitrators, the court said, whereas here the employer had designated a representative, but this representative asserted that the dispute was not arbitrable and therefore refused to participate in selecting a neutral arbitrator. *(Sam Kane Packing Co. v. Meat Cutters)*
- An arbitration award that a union's grievance relating to recall of strikers was not arbitrable could not be vacated by a court where there was no error either in the arbitrator's conclusions or in the procedure by which he reached those conclusions. The parties had agreed to submit the issue of arbitrability to the arbitrator. *(Metal Products Workers v. Torrington Co.)*
- An arbitration award that found an employer in violation of a contract but that reserved jurisdiction to determine the remedy in the future did not constitute a final and binding award that is judicially reviewable. *(Carpenters Local 550 v. Well's Exterior Trim)*
- An arbitrator did not exceed his authority when he excluded polygraph (lie-detector) tests in determining whether an employer had proper cause for discharging two employees suspected of theft. Under the contract, the employer reserved the right to require lie-detector tests of any employee suspected of theft. But the court pointed out that the contract made no mention of the use of such tests in arbitration. Moreover, such tests may be useful in other ways, including preliminary investigation. The arbitrator has great flexibility on the admissibility of evidence, and the court should not review the legal adequacy of his evidentiary rulings, particularly on lie-detector tests—an issue even the courts have found debatable. *(Meat Cutters Local 540 v. Neuhoff Brothers Packers)*

- An arbitrator exceeded his authority in deciding that an employer's past practice of granting employees paid voting time or one hour off on election day was continued during the current contract as an implied condition in view of the employer's failure to negotiate a contrary policy into the contract. *(Torrington Co. v. Auto Workers Local 1645, Metal Products Workers)*
- An arbitrator who found that a supermarket operator had violated the collective bargaining agreement in instituting a new policy to deal with cashiers who forgot to ring up certain purchases exceeded his authority when he created a new policy to replace the one he considered too severe. The contract vested the employer with the right to establish and maintain reasonable rules. *(Bruno's, Inc. v. Food & Commercial Workers Local 1657)*
- The unmistakable public policy favoring the strict observance of federally mandated safety regulations at nuclear power plants requires the vacation of an arbitration award ordering the reinstatement of a nuclear plant employee who deliberately defeated the interlock system controlling the doors of a secondary containment area. *(Iowa Electric Light & Power v. Electrical Workers (IBEW) Local 204)*

9
REGULATION OF UNIONS

Until the adoption of the Landrum-Griffin Act in 1959, Congress had adhered to the view that the Federal Government should not interfere with the internal affairs or organization of labor unions. The courts, both state and federal, had demonstrated a similar aversion to direct intervention in intraunion affairs.

The 1959 Landrum-Griffin or Labor-Management Reporting and Disclosure Act changed all this. It put the Federal Government in the business of policing the internal affairs of labor organizations—local unions as well as national and international bodies. The regulation it provides for is minute in detail.

REPORTING REQUIREMENTS

Labor organizations are required to file two types of reports under the Act. First, every union must adopt a constitution and bylaws and file a copy with the Secretary of Labor. In addition, the union must file a detailed statement of its provisions and procedures with regard to a number of other matters, provided they are not covered in the constitution and bylaws. These include:

- The initiation fee or fees required from a new or transferred member.
- Fees for work permits and the regular dues or fees required to remain a member.

- Qualifications for or restrictions on membership; participation in insurance or other benefit plans.
- Assessments.
- Authorization for disbursement of funds; financial audits.
- The calling of meetings.
- Method of selecting stewards, officers, and delegates, with specific information as to how each present officer got his job.
- Discipline or removal of officers for misconduct.
- Procedure and grounds for imposing fines, suspensions, or expulsions on members.
- Authorization for bargaining demands; ratification of contract terms.
- Strike authorizations.
- Issuance of work permits.

Besides filing all of this information with the Secretary of Labor, a union must make the information available to all of its members. Moreover, it must allow any member who has "just cause" to examine the union's books and records to verify the report.

Financial Reports

The second type of report a union must file under the law is a financial report. Such a report must be filed once a year within 90 days after the close of the union's fiscal year. The report must be signed by the union's president and treasurer and must give the following financial information in reasonable detail:

- Assets and liabilities at the beginning and the end of the year.
- All receipts and their sources.
- Salaries and all other payments to officers and to any employee who received more than $10,000 in total from the union and any of its affiliates.
- Complete information on any loans totaling more than $250 to any officer, employee, or member.

- Complete information on any direct or indirect loans to any business.
- Other disbursements and the reasons for them.

The Department of Labor has issued forms which the unions can use in filing both the information and the financial reports.

The Secretary of Labor may bring civil actions to compel compliance with the reporting requirements. There are criminal penalties for willful violations. Supporting records must be kept available for inspection for five years.

UNION MEMBERS' BILL OF RIGHTS

The Landrum-Griffin Act attempted to legislate into the internal laws and procedures of unions the essential guarantees of the Bill of Rights of the U.S. Constitution. In brief, here is what the provisions seek to guarantee:

Equal Rights

Subject to "reasonable rules and regulations," all union members have equal rights (1) to nominate candidates for union office; (2) to vote in elections or referenda; (3) to attend meetings; and (4) to discuss and vote on matters that come up in union meetings. A union member is defined as anyone who has fulfilled the requirements prescribed by the union for membership. *(Hughes v. Iron Workers Local 11)*

The equal rights guarantee is limited to those rights set forth in the Act and does not include a right to ratify or reject contracts. *(Cleveland Orchestra Committee v. Musicians Local 4)* But if this right is extended to some union members, it may not be arbitrarily denied to others. *(Thomas v. Mine Workers)* The Act does not require a union to hold general membership meetings. *(Grant v. Chicago Truck Drivers)*

Laid-off union members were improperly prohibited from voting on changes in the procedures for recall from layoff, a federal appeals court held, since they were denied their equal right to vote on union matters. The laid-off members were not permitted to pay dues and therefore were not members "in good standing" entitled to vote under the union's constitution, but the court found they were members "in substance." *(Alvey v. General Electric Co.)*

Where a local union violated the union constitution by refusing to permit an employee to transfer his membership to it, the local was ordered to accept the transfer and to pay him damages for loss of wages, injury to his reputation, and humiliation and embarrassment. *(Lusk v. Plumbers Local 540)*

Freedom of Speech and Assembly

This protects the right of members who are opposed to an incumbent administration in a union to meet and make plans to make their opposition effective. It encompasses rights such as that of a local union to have its national union's magazine publish a paid advertisement opposing ratification of a labor agreement which the national had negotiated. *(Knox County Local v. Rural Letter Carriers; cf. Sheldon v. O'Callaghan)* Here again, however, the right is subject to "reasonable rules" of the union—which may, for example, prohibit candidates for office from accepting campaign contributions from nonmembers. *(Steelworkers v. Sadlowski)* And union members do not have an absolute right to access to their union's mailing list. Thus, a union lawfully denied a request by dissident members for access to the the union's mailing list to disseminate their views on a contract proposal. *(Carothers v. Presser)*

The free speech provision protects a member against discipline for expressing his opinion of union officers and policies at union proceedings, even if his statements are false or libelous. *(Salzhandler v. Caputo, Boilermakers v. Rafferty)* He may be subject to a damage action under the common law governing libel and slander, but it has been held that statements made at union proceedings are protected so long as they are not malicious. *(Pulliam v. Bond)*

Counsel fees were appropriately awarded a member who was expelled for introducing resolutions critical of union officers at a membership meeting, the U.S. Supreme Court held. By vindicating his right of free speech, the Court said, he rendered substantial service to the union as an institution and to all its members. *(Hall v. Cole)*

Removal of union officers from their positions for opposing union policies they are supposed to administer does not violate their rights as members to free speech, provided the removal is not an attempt to stifle dissent within the union. *(Newman v. Communications Workers Local 1101)* The same rule has been applied to a union steward at a nuclear power station who was removed from membership on a safety committee. *(Cotter v. Owens)* And union members who hold appointed positions as business agents have no protection against being dismissed from these positions by a new union president whose election they had opposed. *(Finnegan v. Leu)*

Rejecting a claim of preemption by the Taft-Hartley Act, the Supreme Court held that a state-court damage action for infliction of emotional distress could be maintained against a union and its officers by a member who alleged that his complaints about the operation of the union's hiring hall caused him to be subjected to "outrageous conduct," threats, and intimidation. *(Farmer v. Carpenters Local 25)*

A union was liable for damages that a dissident member suffered as a result of a beating he received at a union meeting, a federal appeals court held, where the beating was not a spontaneous incident but was instigated by union leaders to intimidate dissidents in the exercise of their Landrum-Griffin rights. Punitive damages and attorneys' fees were awarded, as well as damages for lost wages and for pain and suffering. *(Shimman v. Frank)*

Dues, Initiation Fees, and Assessments

Before either a local or an international union may raise dues, fees, or assessments, certain procedural safeguards must be met. In a local, the increase must be approved by majority vote in either a special membership meeting or in a membership referendum. Both must be by secret ballot. National and international unions may increase dues, fees, and assessments by majority vote in a regular or special convention, by a secret ballot referendum of the membership, or by majority executive board vote—to be effective until the next convention.

The majority vote requirement was not met when a vote was taken first by a show of hands and then by a standing vote, but no attempt was made to determine the exact division among the voters. *(Rota v. Railway Clerks)*

The majority vote provision establishes only a minimum requirement; a union is free to enact more stringent rules for dues assessments. *(Bunz v. Moving Picture Machine Operators Local 224)*

A union could not lawfully provide for automatic dues increases that were to be commensurate with negotiated wage gains and subject to suspension at the discretion of the union leadership. *(Burroughs v. Operating Engineers Local 3)*

Protection of the Right to Sue

Although a member still must utilize the union's internal procedures before taking a complaint to court, he need do so for only four months. But the exhaustion of the union's internal procedures was not required where the member's complaint did not involve an "internal union matter" *(NLRB v. Marine & Shipbuilding Workers Local 22)*, or where exhaustion would have been futile because the union already had disciplined other members for the same action—crossing a picket line of another union. *(Adamczewski v. Machinists Local 1487)*

The same section also declares a union member to be free "to petition any legislature or to communicate with any legislator."

Safeguards Against Improper Disciplinary Action

Except for failure to pay his dues, no union member may be fined, suspended, or expelled unless he is (1) served with written, specific charges, (2) given a reasonable time to prepare his defense, and (3) afforded a full and fair hearing. But there is no right to legal representation at a disciplinary hearing before the union's full membership. *(Curtis v. Stage Employees Local 125)*

The suspension of a union president from membership and from office was invalidated, where the action was taken by the union's executive council, most of whose members were political enemies of the president. *(Needham v. Isbister)* Similarly, the trial of a member before a panel that includes persons who previously had found him guilty of identical charges does not meet the full and fair hearing requirement. *(Rosario v. Garment Cutters Local 10)*

Any member disciplined in violation of the Act may go to a federal district court for injunctive or other "appropriate" relief. Union members who were fined unlawfully have been awarded compensatory damages for lost wages and for such physical manifestations of emotional distress as loss of sleep and heart palpitations. *(Electrical Workers (IBEW) Local 1969 v. Bise)* Some courts hold that punitive damages may be awarded as well. *(Keene v. Operating Engineers Local 624, Electrical Workers (IBEW) Local 1969 v. Bise)*

Copy of Contract

On request, a local union must give a copy of its collective bargaining contract to any employee whose "rights are directly affected" by the agreement. Labor organizations other than locals must forward copies of contracts to constituent units whose members are directly affected by the agreement. These contracts must be kept at the local's main office and must be available for inspection by anyone whose rights are affected by the agreement.

Local members have been held entitled to copies of contracts with employer associations, including welfare fund and apprentice-training agreements. *(Allen v. Iron Workers Local 92)* A federal district court held that union members do not have a right to copies of union constitutions and bylaws, although the failure to furnish such copies might excuse them from resorting to available union remedies before bringing a court action. *(Forline v. Marble Polishers)*

The Secretary of Labor may enforce the right-to-information provisions of the Act through the federal district courts. Union members also have been found entitled to bring private actions. *(Forline v. Marble Polishers)*

UNION ELECTIONS

National and international unions now are required to elect officers at least once every five years, either by secret ballot among the members or at a convention of delegates chosen by secret ballot. Local unions must elect officers at least once every three years by secret ballot. Officers of intermediate bodies, such as joint councils, must be elected at least once every four years by secret ballot or by delegates who, themselves, were elected by secret ballot.

The Landrum-Griffin Act also lays down some ground rules for the conduct of union elections. Here are some of them:

- A union must comply with any reasonable request by a candidate to distribute campaign literature to members by mail. It cannot discriminate among candidates as to the use of its membership lists for campaign purposes.
- A union may not use money from dues or assessments to promote the candidacy of any person running for union office, even if the amount spent is "minimal." *(Schultz v. Steelworkers Local 6799)* Publication of "officers' reports" in which the retiring union president recommended the election of eight officers has been found violative of the Act. *(Usery v. Stove Workers)* But union money may be used for notices and factual statements of issues not involving candidates and for other election expenses.
- No money of an employer may be used to promote a candidacy for union office. This ban on employer loans and contributions applies even to employers that are not directly affected by the election. *(Marshall v. Teamsters Local 20)*
- Notice of the election must be mailed to each member of the union not less than 15 days prior to the election.
- Reasonable opportunity must be given for the nomination of candidates, and the union must provide adequate

safeguards to assure a fair election, including the right of any candidate to have an observer at the polls and at the counting of ballots.

- Elections must be conducted in accordance with the union's constitution and bylaws, and ballots and election records must be preserved for a year.
- Every member of the union in good standing is entitled to vote and to support candidates of his choice without being subject to penalty, discipline, or reprisal of any kind by the union or any of its members. To be in good standing, a member must have fulfilled the membership requirements, must not have withdrawn voluntarily, and must not have been expelled or suspended in valid proceedings.
- Where officers are elected by delegates at a convention, the union's constitution and bylaws must be observed, and all convention records relating to the election, including credentials of delegates, must be preserved for a year.

Whether a union's election rules are reasonable is decided on a case-by-case basis.

A requirement that a candidate be "competent" to perform the duties of the office sought did not prescribe a "reasonable qualification," an appeals court held. (*Donovan v. Laborers Local 120*) And the Supreme Court has ruled that unions could not require candidates to have held office previously. (*Wirtz v. Hotel & Restaurant Employees Local 6*) or to have attended at least half the union's monthly meetings during the three years before the election. (*Steelworkers Local 3489 v. Usery*) The first restriction eliminated 93 percent of the membership from consideration for office; the second restriction eliminated 96.5 percent.

But the Secretary of Labor may not challenge a union's decision to permit supervisors to run for union office. (*Brock v. Writers Guild*)

ENFORCEMENT OF ELECTION RULES

Up to the point where an election is held, the provisions of state and local laws may be invoked to enforce any rights or remedies that may be available to a member under the union's constitution and bylaws. But once an election has been held, only a union member may initiate an attack on its validity. The Landrum-Griffin Act sets forth a procedure for challenging an election, including a challenge based on alleged infringement of the right to nominate candidates, and it specifies that the remedy thus provided shall be "exclusive." This is the procedure:

- The member must first proceed through the channels provided by the constitution and bylaws of the union and its parent body. But if the internal union procedures do not conform to the requirements of the Act, a court may order a new election. This was done, for example, where a union failed to mail notice of the election to 58 percent of its membership, and only 23 percent voted. *(Brennan v. Teamsters Local 639)*
- The union has three months to handle the complaint. If the union has not acted within that time or if it has acted and the member is not satisfied, he can complain to the Secretary of Labor. He must do so within a month.
- The Secretary must investigate the member's charges. If he finds probable cause to believe that a violation of the law has occurred and has affected the election, he sues to obtain a new election. Any such suit must be limited to the alleged violations the complaining member cited in pursuing his intraunion remedies; the Secretary may not add other alleged violations uncovered in investigating the member's charges. *(Hodgson v. Steelworkers Local 6799)*
- If an election is directed by the court, it then is held under the supervision of the Secretary, who certifies to the court the persons elected. The court then enters a decree declaring them elected.

The Supreme Court held that a challenge to union rules on nomination of candidates was subject to this procedure—the complaining member could not sue on his own. *(Calhoon v. Harvey)* But a union member may intervene in an action by the Secretary of Labor to invalidate an election. *(Trbovich v. Mine Workers)* The Secretary's determination not to sue may be challenged by a defeated candidate, but court review of the Secretary's determination is limited to assuring that the Secretary's decision was rationally based and not arbitrary or capricious. *(Dunlop v. Bachowski)*

Although the Act gives the Secretary exclusive authority to sue to invalidate elections, a successful candidate for local union office was permitted to maintain a tort action for damages against an international union officer who allegedly acted "arbitrarily, recklessly, and with malice and intent to injure" in an effort to deprive the winning candidate of office. *(Ross v. Electrical Workers (IBEW))* A defeated candidate for union office may intervene in a certification proceeding initiated by the Secretary of Labor. Such a candidate, however, must allege that the Secretary has violated the Landrum-Griffin Act or the union's constitution or bylaws in the conduct of the court-ordered election that the Secretary supervised. *(Donovan v. Westside Local 174)*

A federal district court erred when, at the request of dissatisfied union members, it enjoined an ongoing mail-ballot election and ordered a new election under judicially prescribed requirements. This sort of remedy is available only under the statutory postelection procedures, the Supreme Court said, though "less intrusive" remedies might be imposed judicially during the course of the election. *(Teamsters Local 82 v. Crowley)*

REMOVAL OF UNION OFFICERS

The Landrum-Griffin Act places initial reliance on the constitution and bylaws of the local union to provide procedures for the removal of union officers. But the law also instructs the Secretary of Labor to issue rules and regulations prescribing minimum standards and procedures for determining the adequacy of local union removal standards.

The policing of the adequacy of the removal procedures rests with the members of the union. But any member may invoke the aid of the Secretary of Labor in this respect.

The Secretary then is to provide a hearing on the matter. If he finds that the procedures are inadequate for the removal of an elected official guilty of serious misconduct, the official then becomes removable.

Actual removal of an officer has to be accomplished by an election conducted in accordance with the union's constitution and bylaws insofar as they are not inconsistent with the requirements of the Act. Before the election is held, cause must be shown for the officer's removal, and he must be given notice and hearing.

BAN ON FORMER CONVICTS, COMMUNISTS

The Landrum-Griffin Act bars persons convicted of certain crimes from, among other things, holding an office or job with a union or serving as labor relations consultants. Among the crimes covered are robbery, bribery, extortion, embezzlement, grand larceny, burglary, arson, violation of the narcotics laws, murder, rape, assault with intent to kill, assault that inflicts grievous bodily injury, and violation of the law's reporting or trusteeship requirements. A guilty plea followed by a sentence of probation but no judgment under a state's deferred-judgment procedure is considered a conviction for the purposes of this section of the Act. (*Harmon v. Teamsters Local 371*)

The period of debarment is 3 to 13 years, at the discretion of the trial judge. This ban may be lifted, however, if citizenship rights revoked as a result of the conviction are fully restored, or if the U.S. Parole Commission determines that it would not be contrary to the purposes of the law for the individual in question to hold office. Under amendments contained in the Comprehensive Crime Control Act of 1984, incumbent union officers who are convicted of a crime that bars them from office may no longer continue in office while they appeal.

Communists

Under Section 504 of the Landrum-Griffin Act, it was made a crime for a person to hold union office during or for five years after termination of his membership in the Communist Party. This section of the Act was held unconstitutional by the Supreme Court in June 1965 in the *Brown* case.

A provision in a union constitution requiring the expulsion of members who advocate or encourage "communism, facism, nazism, or any other totalitarian philosophy" has been found violative of the Act's free speech guarantees. *(Turner v. Machinists Lodge 1894)*

RULES ON UNION TRUSTEESHIPS

A trusteeship is "any receivership, trusteeship, or other method of supervision or control whereby a labor organization suspends the autonomy otherwise available to a subordinate body under its constitution or bylaws."

Most union constitutions contain procedures for placing local unions under a trusteeship supervised by the parent body. The Landrum-Griffin Act, however, placed some strict controls on such trusteeships.

In the first place, a parent organization that places a local or other subordinate body under trusteeship must file a report on the trusteeship with the Labor Department within 30 days. Thereafter, a report must be filed every six months while the trusteeship remains in effect. Among other things, these reports must give a detailed statement of the reasons for the trusteeship and a full and complete account of the trusteed organization's financial condition when the trusteeship was imposed.

There also are some limitations on the purposes for which a trusteeship may be established. The trusteeship may be imposed only in accordance with the parent organization's constitution and bylaws and only for these purposes:

- Correcting corruption or financial malpractice.
- Assuring the performance of collective bargaining agreements or other duties of a collective bargaining representative.
- Restoring democratic procedures.
- Otherwise carrying out the legitimate objectives of the local.

Unlawful Acts Under Trusteeship

There are certain actions that are forbidden while a subordinate labor organization is under trusteeship. It is unlawful, for example, to count the votes of delegates of a trusteed union in a convention of the parent body unless the delegates have been selected by secret ballot in an election in which all members in good standing of the trusteed union were eligible to vote.

It also is unlawful to transfer to the parent body any current receipts or other funds of the trusteed union, except the normal per capita tax and assessments normally payable.

Willful violation of these restrictions is punishable by a fine of $10,000, a year's imprisonment, or both.

Enforcement of Trusteeship Rules

The Act provides two methods of enforcing the trusteeship requirements:

- A complaint may be made to the Secretary of Labor who, if he finds probable cause to believe a violation has occurred and has not been remedied, may bring civil suit in federal court for such relief as may be appropriate. In such cases, the identity of the complainant is not disclosed.
- A union member or subordinate body "affected by any violation" may bring a civil action for appropriate relief, including an injunction.

In these suits, one of the major considerations will be the length of time the trusteeship has been in effect. If it has been in existence for less than 18 months, it is presumed valid, and relief will be granted only upon "clear and convincing proof" that it was not established or maintained in good faith for a permissible purpose.

But if the trusteeship has been in effect for more than 18 months, the burden shifts and the trusteeship is presumed invalid. The court will decree termination of the trusteeship unless it is shown by "clear and convincing proof" that continuation is necessary for an allowable purpose.

The AFL-CIO was upheld in imposing a trusteeship on the Colorado Labor Council because it endorsed a political candidate, contrary to the AFL-CIO's policy of neutrality. An appeals court ruled that the council was not a labor organization and so the trusteeship provisions were inapplicable. *(Colorado Labor Council v. AFL-CIO)*

RESPONSIBILITIES OF UNION OFFICERS

The Landrum-Griffin Act states that the "officers, agents, shop stewards, and other representatives" of a union occupy positions of trust in relation to the union and its members. The Act specifies three areas in which officers may be held accountable.

Union Funds

Union officers are required to hold, invest, and expend the union's money and property solely for the benefit of the union and its members. Embezzlement of union funds by either a union officer or a union employee is a federal crime punishable by fine, imprisonment, or both.

Conflicts of Interest

Union officers are required to refrain from dealing with the union in an adverse capacity or on behalf of an adverse party in any matter connected with their duties as officers. There also is a breach of trust where a union officer has an investment or other financial or personal interest that conflicts with the interest of the union.

Exploiting the Office

A union officer is required to account to the union for any profits reaped while using his office, although not union funds, to his personal advantage. This type of exploitation is not made a breach of trust, since only an accounting is required. But if the accounting disclosed a conflict of interest, a breach of the fiduciary duty would then be found.

The enforcement of these provisions is left to the union members. As a first step, the member has to complain to the union about an officer's alleged breach of trust. If, after a reasonable time, the union does not do anything about the matter, the member may go into court—state or federal—and ask for leave to sue. If the member shows that he has complied with the law's requirements and shows good cause, he may sue the union officer.

The Act allows a court to award attorneys' fees and to compensate the member for other litigation expenses. But an appeals court held that the attorneys' fees should not be based on the contract between the member and his attorney, but on the value of benefits to the union and the membership. *(Ratner v. Bakery & Confectionery Workers)*

Since union officers have fiduciary duties toward members "even when no monetary interest of the union is involved," they breached their trust when they failed to comply with the contract ratification provision of the union's constitution. *(Stelling v. Electrical Workers (IBEW) Local 1547)* And the fact that payments to union officers were authorized by a vote of the membership is not a complete defense to a charge of breach of fiduciary duty. *(Morrissey v. Curran)*

Union officers breach their fiduciary duty when they appoint individuals to "no show" jobs as organizers *(United States v. Bane)*, and when they refuse, contrary to the members' wishes expressed at a union meeting, to reimburse dissident members for expenses incurred in a successful action to vindicate free speech rights under the Act. *(Johnson v. Nelson)* The fiduciary duty also extends to the handling of pension funds. *(Hood v. Barbers)*

BONDING, EMBEZZLEMENT, LOANS

In addition to imposing a fiduciary responsibility on union officers, the Landrum-Griffin Act also established new rules relating to bonding of union officers and employees, embezzlement of union funds, and loans to union officers. In brief, these are the rules:

- Bonding is required for every officer, agent, shop steward, employee, or other representative of a union who handles funds or other property. The bond may be the typical commercial honesty bond. Bonding also is required for officers or employees of employee benefit funds in which the union "is interested."

- Embezzlement of union funds by a union officer is made a federal offense punishable by a fine of not more than $10,000 or imprisonment for not more than five years, or both. Embezzlement by union employees also is made a criminal offense, although the law does not cover the embezzlement of trust funds in which the union is interested. It also is made a federal offense to use force or threats of force against union members to interfere with the exercise of any of their rights under the Act.

- Loans by a union, directly or indirectly, to either officers or employees of the union are forbidden if they result in a total indebtedness of more than $2,000. Moreover, a union may not pay the fine of any officer or employee convicted of willfully violating the statute; nor may union funds be used to pay the legal fees of officers accused of misappropriating union funds. (*Highway Truck Drivers v. Cohen*) However, the union may reimburse them if their defense is successful (*Holdeman v. Sheldon*), and joint legal representation of the union and its officers may sometimes be permitted. (*Urichuck v. Clark*)

Union officials may be criminally liable for embezzlement if they misuse union property for personal gain, even though the property may not be of any particular value and the union itself stood to gain by their actions. (*United States v. Robinson*)

REPORTS BY UNION OFFICERS

The Landrum-Griffin Act also requires union officers and employees to file reports with the Labor Department on certain financial holdings and transactions. The reports must be filed annually within 90 days of the end of the fiscal year in which the transaction occurred. They must cover not only the official or employee but also his wife and minor children, and they must describe:

- Any stock or other financial interest in any company represented or being organized by the union.
- Any payment or benefit from the company other than wages and benefits earned as a bona fide employee.
- Any transaction involving the stock or other financial interest in the company.
- Any stock or other financial interest in a company that does a substantial part of its business with an employer represented by or being organized by the union, and any income or other benefits received from such a company.
- Any stock or other financial interest in a company that deals in any way with the union.
- Any business transaction or arrangement with a company represented or being organized by the union, except pay for bona fide employment or purchases or sales in the normal course of business at regular prices.
- Payments or other benefits received from a labor relations consultant, other than specified permitted payments for legitimate purposes.

Exceptions

There are exceptions for bona fide investments in securities traded on a registered national exchange and in shares of registered investment companies and public utility holding companies. No report is required if the officer and his family had no dealings of the kind listed.

Enforcement

The Secretary of Labor is empowered to enforce these requirements by civil actions in the federal courts. There are criminal penalties for willful violations. Records supporting a report must be kept available for inspection for five years.

RESTRICTIONS ON EMPLOYERS, CONSULTANTS

The Landrum-Griffin Act placed some new restrictions on the activities of employers and labor relations consultants.

The restrictions on employers relate primarily to certain payments to employees and to union officers or agents. Some types of payments are made illegal, and employers also are required to file reports with the Secretary of Labor regarding certain payments and arrangements.

Unlawful Payments

Section 302 of the Taft-Hartley Act made it unlawful for an employer to make payments, with certain exceptions, to "any representative of any of his employees." It also was made unlawful for the representative to demand or accept such payments.

The Landrum-Griffin Act broadened these provisions considerably. The ban was expanded to include payments made by employer associations, labor relations consultants acting for an employer, and anyone else who acts in the employer's interest. It also was broadened to include loans or agreements to lend, as well as payments of money or any other thing of value.

Under the Taft-Hartley Act, only payments to a representative of the employer's employees were unlawful. Now the category of recipients has been expanded so that payments or loans are unlawful if they go to any of the following:

- Any representative of the employer's employees.
- Unions and union officers or employees where the union is seeking to represent the employer's employees or would admit them to membership.
- Any union officer or employee if the employer's intent is to influence him in respect to any of his actions or decisions as a union officer or employee.
- Individual employees or employee committees if (1) the payment is in excess of the employee's normal compensation and (2) it is for the purpose of causing the employee or employee committee directly or indirectly to influence other employees with respect to their organizing or bargaining rights.

An appeals court ruled that Section 302 was violated when a union president asked an employer to make weekly payments to a third party who performed no services for the company—however, this was despite the absence of proof that the union president received any of this money. *(United States v. DeBrouse)* A violation was also found where an employer made payments, mainly in the form of salaries paid to a succession of no-show employees over the course of a decade, to a union's business agent. *(United States v. Pecora)*

Exempted Payments

There are a number of specific exemptions from this ban on employer payments or loans. They include: (1) compensation paid to a union officer or employee by reason of his services as an employee of the employer and payments to any employee whose duties include acting openly for the employer in labor relations or personnel matters; (2) payments to satisfy or settle a legal judgment, administrative agency order, or arbitration award; (3) the purchase of an article at the prevailing market price; (4) the deduction and payment of union dues pursuant to a checkoff agreement; (5) payments into an employee benefit trust fund that meets certain specifications; and (6) payments to a trust fund established for the purpose of pooled vacation, holiday, severance, or similar benefits or to defray the costs of apprenticeship or other training programs, provided certain conditions are met.

These exceptions did not legalize employer payments to a fund that was established by agreement between a union and three employer associations which paid the salary and expenses of a steward responsible for investigating employer compliance with the agreement. The appeals court held that the steward was not an "employee" of the contracting employers. *(Iron Workers Local 426 v. Bechtel Power Corp.)* Pension fund contributions that an employer made on behalf of individuals who took leaves of absence to accept full-time positions with a union were also found to be unlawful. *(Trailways Lines v. Trailways, Inc. Joint Council)*

But a no-docking provision of a contract, which requires an employer to allow union officials time off with pay to conduct union-related business other than direct meetings with the employer's management, is not unlawful under Section 302. *(BASF Wyandotte Corp. v. Chemical Workers Local 227)*

REPORTING REQUIREMENTS

Unlike unions, employers are not required by the Landrum-Griffin Act to file any regular reports with the Labor Department. They must file reports only if they make certain payments or enter into certain arrangements. The reports are due within 90 days after the end of the employer's fiscal year in which the payments or arrangements were made.

A report is required on any of the following kinds of transactions or arrangements:

- Payments or loans to any union or its representative, except those made by a bank, credit union, or other lending agency and those—such as normal wages—that are permitted by the unlawful payment provisions.
- Secret payments to certain employees to get them to persuade other employees on matters of organizing or bargaining.
- Expenditures intended to interfere with the right of employees to bargain freely.
- Expenditures for information on activities of employees or a union in connection with a labor dispute involving the employer, except for use in a proceeding before an arbitrator, administrative agency, or a court.
- Any arrangement with a labor consultant or other outsider where an object is to persuade employees with respect to organizing or collective bargaining.
- Any arrangement with a labor consultant or other outsider where an object is to get information on the activities of employees or a union in connection with a labor dispute involving the company, except for use in a proceeding before an arbitrator, administrative agency, or court.
- Any payment made pursuant to such arrangements with consultants or other outsiders.

Reports by Consultants

The reporting requirements with respect to the last three types of arrangements and payments listed above are two-edged. The consultant, as well as the employer, must file a report on the arrangement or payment. The consultant's report on an arrangement must be filed within 30 days after it is made. Reports on payments or disbursements under an arrangement must be filed annually.

The consultant, however, need not file reports for the following types of services: (1) giving of advice to an employer; (2) representing an employer before a court, administrative agency, or arbitration tribunal; and (3) negotiating bargaining agreements or grievances. Furthermore, attorneys need not report information lawfully communicated to them by clients in the course of a legitimate attorney-client relationship.

The Labor Department, however, has taken the position that where an attorney, or consultant, enters into any arrangement during a year to persuade employees with respect to organizing or collective bargaining, he must file a report on all income and expenditures during the year in connection with labor relations advice and services, not merely those related to the persuasion activities. This view has been upheld by four appeals courts. (*Douglas v. Wirtz, Price v. Wirtz, Master Printers Association v. Donovan, Humphreys, Hutcheson & Moseley v. Donovan*) A fifth appeals court disagrees. (*Donovan v. Rose Law Firm*)

These reporting and financial-disclosure requirements have been imposed on a printers trade association that distributed antiunion literature to its members' employees. (*Master Printers of America v. Donovan*)

Enforcement

The Secretary of Labor may bring a civil action in court whenever it appears that any employer or consultant has violated or is about to violate the reporting requirements. There are criminal penalties for willful violations. All of the reports required under the law—from unions, union officers, employers, and consultants—are available for inspection by interested persons at the Labor Department. Records supporting the reports must be kept available for inspection for five years.

TAFT-HARTLEY ACT RESTRICTIONS

It is an unfair labor practice under the Taft-Hartley Act for a union to restrain or coerce employees in the exercise of their rights under the Act, including the right to refrain from union or concerted activities. Decisions construing this prohibition have held as follows:

- A union did not violate the Act when it fined members for crossing a lawful picket line set up by the union or when it instituted a legal proceeding to collect the fines. *(NLRB v. Allis-Chalmers Manufacturing Co.)*
- A union violated the Act when it fined employees who had been members in good standing but who resigned and returned to work during a lawful strike called by the union. *(NLRB v. Textile Workers Local 1029)*
- A union may not restrict the right of its members to resign. *(Machinists Local Lodge 1414 (Neufeld Porsche-Audi))*
- A union may not prohibit resignations in anticipation of or during the pendency of charges of union misconduct. *(NLRB v. Sheet Metal Workers Local 73)*
- A union unlawfully fined former members who returned to work after resigning from the union during a strike, even though the union's constitution prohibited resignations during or just before a strike. *(Pattern Makers League v. NLRB (Rockford-Beloit Pattern Jobbers))*
- The NLRB does not have authority to determine whether a fine lawfully imposed on a member is "reasonable" in amount; this is a matter for the state courts to determine. *(NLRB v. Boeing Co.)*
- A union lawfully fined members for drawing immediate piecework pay for work in excess of a union-initiated production ceiling. *(Scofield v. NLRB)* But a union violated its bargaining duty by enforcing a production ceiling that in effect resulted in employees' working less than the

workweek prescribed by their collective bargaining contract. *(Painters District Council No. 9 v. NLRB)*

- A union unlawfully expelled a member for failing to exhaust the intraunion grievance procedure before filing a charge against the union with the NLRB. *(NLRB v. Marine & Shipbuilding Workers Local 22)*

- Unions lawfully suspended or expelled members for filing petitions with the NLRB to decertify the unions. *(Tawas Tube Products, Inc., Price v. NLRB)* But a union violated the Act when it fined—rather than suspended or expelled—a member who had filed a decertification petition. *(NLRB v. Molders Local 125)*

- A union lawfully may threaten disciplinary action, including expulsion, against members if they do not assist, or actively oppose, its organizing campaign. *(Meat Cutters Local 593)*

- An international union, district lodge, and local union unlawfully cancelled an employee's membership without notice because he had engaged in internal union activities critical of the incumbent administration. The NLRB properly ordered publication of its notice detailing the union's unlawful conduct in the international union's journal. *(NLRB v. Machinists Lodge No. 707)*

- A union lawfully removed the chairman of its plant safety committee from his position for supporting the losing candidate for the union presidency. His interest in retaining his position is outweighed by the union's interest in placing in office those members who it considers would best serve the union and its membership. *(Shenango, Inc.)*

- A union rule denying strike benefits to any striker if he or his spouse is "scabbing" at a struck plant is lawful, even though the "scabbing" spouse is not a union member. *(Food & Commercial Workers Local 222)*

- A union that unlawfully brought intraunion charges against members is liable for lost wages, travel, and other expenses the members incurred in attending the union trial. *(Laborers District Council (Hayward Baker Co.))*

The Taft-Hartley Act also makes it unlawful for a union to restrain or coerce an employer in the selection of its representatives for the purposes of collective bargaining or the adjustment of grievances. This prohibition arises in the disciplining of supervisor-members. Supreme Court rulings on this prohibition include:

- A union lawfully disciplined supervisor-members for working for employers that did not have collective bargaining contracts with the union, since the supervisors did not have grievance-adjustment or collective bargaining responsibilities and their employer had not entered into and did not seek a collective bargaining contract with the union. *(NLRB v. Electrical Workers (IBEW) Local 340)*
- A union's discipline is only unlawful when it adversely affects the supervisor's conduct as a grievance adjuster or collective bargainer on behalf of an employer. A union may fine or expel from membership a supervisor-member for crossing a picket line and performing struck work during a lawful strike, the Court said. *(Florida Power & Light Co. v. Electrical Workers (IBEW))*
- A union unlawfully fined supervisors who performed grievance-adjustment duties during a strike. *(American Broadcasting Cos. v. Writers Guild)*

Rulings of the NLRB and appeals courts include the following:

- The NLRB will uphold union discipline if a supervisor-member performs more than a minimal amount of rank-and-file work during a strike. *(Columbia ITU Union 101)*
- A union unlawfully disciplined three supervisor-members for performing their supervisory duties during a lockout. *(NLRB v. Operating Engineers Local 501)*

Union Affiliation Election

A union is not required to permit nonmembers to vote in a union affiliation election, the Supreme Court ruled, reversing the NLRB. The decision of a union to alter its affiliation remains an internal union matter free from outside interference unless the Board determines that the affiliation raises doubts about the union's representative status. *(NLRB v. Financial Institution Employees (Seattle-First National Bank))*

10

HOW TO USE THE TAFT-HARTLEY ACT

How may employees, unions, or employers who believe their rights under the law have been violated obtain redress?

What may employees or employers do to clear up the situation when there is a controversy over which union, if any, is entitled to deal with an employer on behalf of his employees?

Before these and similar questions can be answered, it first is necessary to take a careful look at how the Taft-Hartley Act and the NLRB operate.

TWO TYPES OF LABOR LAWS

When it comes to enforcement, laws regulating labor-management relations are of two general kinds. One creates an agency to enforce the law. The Taft-Hartley Act belongs to this class. The other leaves it to the aggrieved party to bring action in the courts. The Railway Labor Act is an example of this type.

Under the Fair Labor Standards Act, both the Labor Department and aggrieved employees may bring court actions. Title VII of the Civil Rights Act also provides for suits both by the Equal Employment Opportunity Commission and by aggrieved individuals. The same is true under the Age Discrimination in Employment Act. But the government officials must attempt to resolve the dispute by conference, persuasion, and conciliation

155

before authorizing a suit by an individual or a class action by a number of persons.

Sometimes agencies set up to enforce laws are known as quasi-judicial agencies—meaning that they are similar to courts in some respects. In other respects, they resemble the office of state attorney, being charged with the duty of prosecuting offenses on behalf of the government. So these agencies have two duties—(1) to prosecute violations, and (2) to judge whether a violation has occurred, and, if it has, to prescribe remedies.

SEPARATING PROSECUTOR FROM JUDGE

These two duties are present in all quasi-judicial agencies. In the case of the National Labor Relations Board, however, the two duties are separated more completely than in the case of any like body. The way this is done is rather complicated.

First, there is the Board itself. It consists of five members appointed by the President with the advice and consent of the Senate. It is essentially the judicial branch of the agency.

Second, there is the Board's General Counsel, also appointed by the President with the advice and consent of the Senate. The title is misleading because he does not advise the Board on points of law. This is done by the Solicitor of the Board. The General Counsel is the prosecutor. As such, he listens to charges that the law has been violated and determines which of the cases brought to him he should prosecute before the Board. If he decides not to prosecute a charge, it is virtually impossible to obtain review of his action.

FACT-FINDING DUTIES

The NLRB and its General Counsel are more than an enforcement agency, however. They have fact-finding duties also. These include determining the bargaining agent employees in a bargaining unit want to represent them and determining whether employees wish to get rid of a bargaining agent or a union-shop contract.

The General Counsel is entrusted by the Board with the duty of arranging for elections on these questions. The actual work is entrusted to the Board's regional offices, which the General Counsel supervises. The Board has delegated to its regional directors decision-making authority in election cases, subject to certain exceptions and possible review by the Board.

PROCEDURES ILLUSTRATED

It is possible to see how the Act operates in practice by taking two typical cases and following the steps as they take place. One case will arise from a charge of unfair labor practices; the other from a dispute as to bargaining agent. Although everything does not always happen the same way, the picture is roughly accurate.

DISCHARGE OF EMPLOYEE

Suppose an employee who has joined a union is discharged. He and the union officials may believe that the motive for his discharge was based on his having joined the union and that he is being made an example of as a means of discouraging others from joining. Acting through the union, he files a charge at the nearest regional office of the NLRB. Forms are provided for use in making the charge.

At this point, the employer first comes into contact with a Board agent, usually through a telephone call asking for an interview. One is arranged. It is possible the agent may be convinced that there has been a misunderstanding and that some other good reason existed for the discharge. But he will reach this conclusion only after he has satisfied himself by an investigation that it is true. He has authority to come into the plant, require access to records, and make whatever inquiries he may consider necessary.

The episode may end by dismissal of the charge by the regional director, although the union still may appeal to the General Counsel from the dismissal. But if the regional director believes that there is possible ground for the charge, the outcome will be different. In that case, the employer may decide to reinstate the employee. Otherwise, the regional director will issue a formal complaint against the employer charging him with violating the law.

(If the unfair labor practice charge is against a union and involves certain types of strikes, picketing, or boycotts, the General Counsel may be required to obtain an injunction against the conduct pending a decision by the Board in the case. See Chapter 7. The General Counsel has discretion as to whether to seek an injunction in other types of unfair labor practice cases.)

The Formal Proceeding

If settlement efforts fail, a formal proceeding begins. A hearing is arranged before an administrative law judge. The employer is confronted with the complaint and is given an opportunity to disprove the allegations, if possible. His adversary is an attorney from the office of the General Counsel, whose aim it is to convince the administrative law judge that the charges are supported by the facts. Witnesses testify and are cross-examined and the administrative law judge then makes his decision.

Whatever the law judge's decision, each side may be given an opportunity to argue before the Board for or against it. The Board makes its decision which may be in the form of findings of fact, conclusions of law, and an order. The order may be a dismissal of the complaint. But more frequently it requires the employer to cease and desist from an unfair labor practice he is found to have committed. Additional orders, designed to undo the effects of the unfair practice, may be issued. These may include a requirement that the employer reinstate the employee with or without back pay. This ends the Board stage of the enforcement procedure.

Since the 1947 amendments to the Act, the Board also has policed unfair labor practices by unions. The 1959 Landrum-Griffin Act added to the restrictions. In the case of secondary boycotts and certain types of picketing, the Board is required to go to court and seek an injunction against the union's action.

Enforcement of Order

A short period is allowed for compliance before the next stage is begun—appeal to the courts. The court proceeding may be initiated in two ways: the Board may ask a federal court of appeals to enforce the order or the employer may ask the court to set the order aside.

If the court decides to enforce the order, then for the first time the employer feels the force of compulsion to comply. Failure to do so may bring contempt of court proceedings, with possible fine and imprisonment. There, of course, may be appeal to the Supreme Court of the United States.

When the courts are asked to enforce or set aside an order of the Board, the scales are weighed in favor of the Board. The Act requires the courts to accept the facts as found by the Board if they are supported by substantial evidence on the record considered as a whole. The Supreme Court, however, has said that this does not mean that the courts may not take into account contradictory evidence or evidence from which conflicting inferences could be drawn. The substantiality of evidence, it added, must take into account whatever in the record fairly detracts from its weight. (*Universal Camera Corp. v. NLRB*)

Contempt Proceeding

A decree of a court enforcing an order of the Board is in effect a continuing injunction. Enforcement of the decree thus becomes the province of the court. This may be called the third stage of the enforcement of the law. It operates through the bringing of contempt proceedings by the Board.

This stage differs from earlier stages in that the court is its own fact finder. The court, moreover, may draw its own inferences from the facts and prescribe remedies without regard to the views of the Board.

REPRESENTATION DISPUTE

The second kind of dispute involves the NLRB's fact-finding powers. It occurs when a union wants to be recognized as bargaining agent, but the employer wishes first to be assured that the union represents a majority of the employees in the appropriate unit. In such a case, the employer may wait for the union to take the initiative by filing a petition for certification or charges of refusal to bargain. But the employer also may take the initiative himself by filing a petition for an election with the Board.

Assuming that the employer takes the initiative, he obtains from the Board's regional office a form to complete, in which he enters information called for, including a statement that the union wishes to represent certain classifications of employees. After the regional office of the Board gets the form, it sends an official to look into the situation. If the official is satisfied that the employer's business affects interstate commerce and there is no obvious obstacle to an election, such as a valid contract with another union, he will call in the union and try to get an agreement between the employer and the union as to the unit of employees to be represented and as to other details.

If an agreement is reached, a consent election employing informal procedures will be conducted, the ballot providing for the choice of the union or for no union. If the union wins, it is declared bargaining agent and is certified as such.

If no agreement is reached between the union and employer, formal procedures are utilized. There is a hearing before a hearing officer, and findings are made as to the appropriate unit and whether to conduct an election. Even after the election has been held there may be challenges to ballots and election objections to be disposed of before any certification may be issued. The rules on these phases of the proceeding are discussed in detail in Chapter 4.

REVIEW OF DETERMINATIONS, SETTLEMENTS

Ordinarily determinations by the Board regarding bargaining units and bargaining agents are final, except as they may be reviewed in later refusal-to-bargain proceedings as arbitrary or lacking substantial evidence as a base. But the Supreme Court has held that the immunity from direct court review does not apply where the Board determination violates the terms of the

Act itself, such as by including professional employees in a unit with nonprofessionals without the majority approval of the professionals. *(Leedom v. Kyne)* However, the Court held in 1964 that a federal district court could not enjoin an election directed by the Board notwithstanding the company's claim that it was not the employer of the employees involved. *(Boire v. Greyhound Corp.)*

An informal settlement reached after an unfair labor practice complaint is issued but before an NLRB hearing begins is not subject to judicial review, the Supreme Court ruled, even if the party that filed the underlying charge refused to join in the settlement. *(NLRB v. Food & Commercial Workers Local 23 (Charley Bros.))*

JURISDICTIONAL DISPUTE PROCEEDINGS

With the objective of protecting employers against being caught in the middle of union disputes over job assignments, Section 8(b)(4)(D) of the Taft-Hartley Act made it an unfair labor practice for a union to attempt by picketing or striking to force an employer to assign work to one group of employees rather than to another. But Congress declined to rely solely on the machinery provided to remedy other unfair labor practices and added a unique preliminary step for the handling of Section 8(b)(4)(D) disputes. Section 10(k) provides that before passing on the unfair practice charge, the NLRB must first "determine the dispute" unless the parties have adjusted or agreed upon methods for voluntary adjustment of the dispute.

A method of adjustment binding only on the unions involved does not deprive the Board of jurisdiction to determine the dispute since the employer is one of the "parties" to the dispute. *(NLRB v. Plasterers Local 79)*

In making a "determination of the dispute," the Board for several years confined itself merely to determining whether the striking union was lawfully entitled to compel assignment of the work to its members by virtue of a contract or NLRB certification. It refrained from making an affirmative award of the disputed work. In 1961, however, the U.S. Supreme Court told the Board that its policy was not the correct one. The Court said that where two or more unions are claiming the right to perform work and the case is brought before the Board, it is the Board's duty to decide which group is right "and then specifically to award such tasks in accordance with its decision." The Board now makes such work jurisdiction awards. *(NLRB v. Radio Engineers Local 1212, Machinists Lodge 1743)*

But where the factors traditionally relied on do not favor an exclusive award to either union, the Board will preserve in the employer the right to assign the work. *(Machinists Lodge 70, Harley-Davidson Motor Co.)*

An unfair labor practice proceeding is instituted in these jurisdictional strike cases where (1) private adjustment machinery exists but has broken down or (2) a Section 10(k) determination has been issued, but the parties have not complied with the finding. A ruling in the unfair practice proceeding is enforceable in the U.S. courts of appeals.

There are two other types of proceedings conducted by the Board—the decertification election and the union-shop deauthorization election. These are discussed in Chapters 4 and 6.

RULE-MAKING PROCEEDING

Although the Board had been under pressure for several years to utilize its rule-making powers in establishing rules of general application, it did not invoke its rule-making powers until late 1970. The issue was the establishment of annual revenue standards for the assertion of jurisdiction over private universities and colleges. In establishing the standards, the Board followed the rules of the Administrative Procedure Act and held a formal hearing at which interested parties were permitted to present evidence. *(NLRB Rule making power under APA)*

The Board also has used its rule-making power in asserting jurisdiction over symphony orchestras and in refusing to assert jurisdiction in the horse- and dog-racing industries. It has also issued a proposed rule for establishing bargaining units in the health-care industry. *(NLRB Rule making power under APA)*

GLOSSARY OF LABOR TERMS

The current language of labor relations in the United States reflects the later steps of a transitional stage.

Many of the words used in describing events arising from the employer-employee relationship took on their present meaning in an environment of conflict, often breaking out into a form of private warfare.

The newer words are mainly those closely associated with the language of laws and governmental agencies. They bear witness to an increasing element of governmental regulation to replace the more or less open hostility of earlier days.

The definitions which follow are intended as a guide in the understanding of talk or writing on industrial relations.

Many of the words have generally understood meanings outside of their usage in the labor field. In this glossary, however, only those meanings are given which are peculiar to their usage in labor relations.

Administrative law judge Official who conducts hearings and makes recommendations to the NLRB or other government agency. (Formerly called a trial or hearing examiner.)

Affecting commerce Test of application of the Taft-Hartley Act. If a business is such that a labor dispute would threaten interruption of or burden interstate commerce, the jurisdiction of the National Labor Relations Board comes into play.

Affirmative order Command issued by a labor relations board requiring the persons found to have engaged in unfair labor practices to take such steps as will, so far as possible, undo the effect of such practices.

Agency shop A contract provision requiring nonmembers

of the contracting union to pay to the union or a designated charity a sum equal to union dues.

Agent Person acting for an employer or a union; act of the agent implicates the principal for whom the agent acts in the matter of unfair labor practices or of conduct subject to court action whether or not specifically authorized or approved.

All-union shop A term sometimes applied to arrangement more specifically described by the terms closed shop or union shop. See *Closed shop, Union shop.*

Annual improvement factor Annual wage increase, fixed in advance as to amount, and granted on the premise that the employees are entitled to share in the long-term increase in the productivity of a company or industry.

Annual wage Wages paid under terms that guarantee a specified minimum for the year or a minimum period of employment for the year.

Anticertification strike Strike designed to force an employer to cease recognizing a union which has been certified as bargaining agent and to recognize the striking union instead. This is an unfair labor practice under the Taft-Hartley Act as to which a court injunction must be asked if it is believed that a complaint should be issued.

Anti-closed-shop laws See *Right to work.*

Anti-injunction acts Federal and state statutes that limit the jurisdiction of courts to issue injunctions in labor disputes. See *Injunction.*

Antitrust laws Federal and state statutes to protect trade and commerce from unlawful restraints and monopolies. For many years, they were used to restrict union activities such as strikes, picketing, and boycotts. In recent years, however, their use in labor cases has been limited by statute and judicial interpretation.

Appropriate unit See *Unit.*

Arbitration Method of deciding a controversy under which parties to the controversy have agreed in advance to accept the award of a third party.

Authorization card A statement signed by employee designating a union as authorized to act as his agent in collective bargaining.

Automation Term used by industrial engineers to describe mechanical materials handling and the new computer technology that can automate entire factories. It sometimes is used loosely to describe any technological improvement.

Back pay Wages required to be paid to employees who have been discharged in violation of a legal right, either one based on a law or acquired by contract.

Back-to-work movement Organized effort to reopen a struck plant, participated in by employees opposed to the strike and by the business community, sometimes with police aid.

Bargaining unit See *Unit*.

Blacklist List of names of persons or firms to be discriminated against, either in the matter of employment or patronage. See *Unfair list*.

Board of inquiry Body to be appointed by President to mediate and report in national emergency disputes under the Taft-Hartley Act.

Bona fide union A union chosen or organized freely by employees without unlawful influence on the part of their employer.

Bootleg contract A collective bargaining agreement which is contrary to the policy of the Taft-Hartley Act, such as a closed shop. Enforcement of such contracts may eventually entail back-pay awards, but this risk is sometimes considered outweighed by the advantages of avoiding a strike.

Boycott Refusal to deal with or buy the products of a business as a means of exerting pressure in a labor dispute.

Bureau of Labor Statistics Bureau in the Labor Department that issues statistics concerning labor relations, including the Consumer Price Index to which some wage adjustments are tied.

Business agent Paid representative of a local union who handles its grievance actions and negotiations with employers, enrolling of new members, and other membership and general business affairs. Sometimes called a walking delegate.

Captive audience Employees required to attend a meeting in which an employer makes an antiunion speech shortly before an election. Now an employer need give the union an opportunity to answer such a speech under similar conditions only if he enforces a broad no-solicitation rule.

Card check Checking union authorization cards signed by employees against employer's payroll to determine whether union represents a majority of the employer's employees.

Casual workers Persons irregularly employed.

Cease-and-desist order A command issued by a labor relations board requiring employer or union to abstain from unfair labor practice.

Central labor union Federation of union locals in one city or county having affiliations with different national unions but same parent body.

Certification Official designation by a labor board of a labor organization entitled to bargain as exclusive representative of employees in a certain unit. See *Unit*.

Charge Formal allegation against employer or union under labor relations acts on the basis of which, if substantiated, a complaint may be issued by a board or commission.

Checkoff Arrangement under which an employer deducts from pay of employees the amount of union dues and turns over the proceeds to the treasurer of the union.

Closed shop Arrangement between an employer and a union under which only members of the union may be hired. See *Union shop*.

Coalition (Coordinated) bargaining Joint or cooperative efforts by a group of unions in negotiating contracts with an employer who deals with a number of unions.

Coercion Economic or other pressure exerted by an employer to prevent the free exercise by employees of their right to self-organization and collective bargaining; intimidation by union or fellow employees to compel affiliation with union.

Collective bargaining Negotiations looking toward a labor contract between an organization of employees and their employer or employers.

Collective bargaining contract Formal agreement over wages, hours, and conditions of employment entered into between an employer or group of employers and one or more unions representing employees of the employers.

Company police Deputized police officers paid by an employer to protect his premises but used also at times to combat strikers or pickets.

Company town Towns in which the land and houses are owned by a company which is the sole or chief employer in the town.

Company union Organizations of employees of a single employer usually with implication of employer domination.

Concerted activities Activities undertaken jointly by employees for the purpose of union organization, collective bargaining, or other mutual aid or protection. Such activities are "protected" under the Taft-Hartley Act.

Conciliation Efforts by third party toward the accommodation of opposing viewpoints in a labor dispute so as to effect a voluntary settlement.

Condonation rule An employer may be held in some instances to have "condoned" unprotected employees' activities and thereby waived the right to discharge or discipline these employees.

Consent decree Court order entered with the consent of the parties.

Consent election Election held by a labor board after informal hearing in which various parties agree on terms under which the election is to be held.

Constructive discharge Unfavorable treatment of employee marked for discharge so that employee will "voluntarily" resign.

Consumer picketing Picketing of a retail store in which the pickets urge customers not to patronize the store or to buy a particular product. If the picketing is in support of a strike against a producer or supplier, the picketing is legal if it is aimed merely at getting customers not to buy products of the struck employer. It is unlawful if it is aimed at getting the customers to stop patronizing the store entirely.

Consumer Price Index An index prepared monthly by the Labor Department's Bureau of Labor Statistics measuring changes in prices of a specific "market basket" of commodities and services. It is significant in labor relations because wage escalation under some collective bargaining contracts is tied to the index.

Contract-bar rules Rules applied by the NLRB in determining when an existing contract between an employer and a union will bar a representation election sought by a rival union.

Contracting out See *Subcontracting*.

Cooling-off period Period during which employees are forbidden to strike under laws which require a definite period of notice before a walkout.

Cost-of-living adjustment (COLA) Collective bargaining contracts often contain "escalator" clauses that require wage or salary adjustments at stated intervals in a ratio linked to changes in the Consumer Price Index.

Craft union Labor organization admitting to membership persons engaged in a specified type of work, usually involving a special skill.

Craft unit Bargaining unit consisting of workers following a particular craft or using a particular type of skill, such as molders, carpenters, etc. The NLRB may rule that a craft unit, often included in a broad industrial unit of production-and-maintenance employees, may be split off from the larger unit and bargain separately. The election to determine whether the craft workers desire separate representation is a craft-severance election.

Damage suits Suits which may be brought in federal courts, without the usual limitations, to recover damages for breach of collective bargaining contracts and for violation of prohibitions against secondary boycotts and other unlawful strike action under the Taft-Hartley Act.

Deauthorization election Election held by the NLRB under the Taft-Hartley Act to determine whether employees wish to deprive their union bargaining agent of authority to bind them under a union-shop contract.

Decertification Withdrawal of bargaining agency from union upon vote by employees in unit that they no longer wish to be represented by union.

Discharge Permanent separation of employee from payroll by employer.

Discrimination Short form for "discrimination in regard to hire or tenure of employment as a means of encouraging or discouraging membership in a labor organization"; also refusal to hire, promote, or admit to union membership because of race, creed, color, sex, or national origin.

Discriminatory discharge Discharge for union activity, or because of race, color, religion, sex, or national origin.

Disestablishment Remedy ordered by the NLRB when it finds that an employer has dominated a labor organization. The employer is ordered to cease recognizing the labor organization, to disestablish it, and to post notices informing employees it will not recognize, support, or encourage the dominated union.

Domination Control exercised by an employer over a union of his employees.

Double-breasted Operating both on a unionized and nonunion basis. This form of operation is found particularly in the construction industry, where a unionized employer may form a nonunion subsidiary to meet competition from nonunion companies.

Dual union Labor organization formed to enlist members among workers already claimed by another union.

Economic strike Strike not caused by unfair labor practice of an employer.

Election See *Employee election.*

Emergency board Body appointed under Railway Labor Act

by President of the United States when a strike or lockout is imminent on interstate railroads. See *Board of inquiry*.

Emergency dispute A labor dispute in which a strike would imperil the national health and safety. Special procedures are provided under the Taft-Hartley Act for dealing with such disputes.

Employee association A term sometimes used for plant union.

Employee election Balloting by employees for the purpose of choosing a bargaining agent or unseating one previously recognized. See *Referendum*.

Employee representation plan System under which employees select representatives to a joint body on which the management is also represented, the purpose of the body being to discuss grievances or company policy.

Employer association Organization of employers in related enterprises, usually acting together in labor policy or bargaining as a unit with one or more unions.

Employer unit Bargaining unit consisting of all production and maintenance employees working for one employer.

Employment at will Doctrine under which employees may be discharged for whatever reason their employer chooses, absent some con-

tractual or statutory limitation. Many jurisdictions now recognize exceptions to the at-will doctrine.

Employment contract Agreement entered into between an employer and one or more employees. See *Collective bargaining contract, Individual contract*.

Escape period A period, normally 15 days, during which employees may resign from a union so as not to be bound to continue membership under membership maintenance agreements.

Espionage Practice of spying on employees with a view to discovering membership in, or activity for, labor organizations.

Exactions Payment under more or less direct duress for work not done and not intended to be done. Under the Taft-Hartley Act, seeking exactions is an unfair labor practice and making or receiving such payments is a crime for employers and unions or individuals.

Extortionate picketing Picketing for the personal profit or enrichment of an individual, except through a bona fide increase in wages or other employee benefits, by taking or obtaining any money or other thing of value from the employer against his will or with his consent. Such picketing was made a federal crime by the Labor-Management Reporting and Disclosure Act.

Fact-finding boards Agencies appointed, usually by a government official, to determine facts and make recommendations in major disputes. See *Board of inquiry*.

Fair employment practice Term applied in some statutes to conduct which does not contravene prohibitions against discrimination in employment because of race, color, religion, sex, or national origin.

Featherbedding Contractual requirements that employees be hired in jobs for which their services are not needed. See *Exactions*.

Free riders A term sometimes applied by unions to nonmembers within the unit represented by the union, the implication being that they obtain without cost the benefits of a contract obtained through the efforts of the dues-paying members.

Free speech The right of employers to express views hostile to unionization, provided no threat of coercion or promise of benefit is contained therein. If the expression of views is coercive, it becomes unlawful interference with employees' rights.

Freeze order Government order freezing wages, salaries, prices, and rents as of a particular date, such as issued during the Korean War and in August 1971.

Fringe benefits Term used to encompass items such as vacations, holidays, insurance, medical benefits, pensions, and other similar benefits that are given to an employee under his employment or union contract in addition to direct wages. Increasingly referred to as "employee benefits" or as "nonwage compensation."

Furlough Period of layoff.

General Counsel Officer of the National Labor Relations Board whose chief duty is to issue and prosecute complaints in unfair labor practice cases presented to the Board for decision.

Good-faith bargaining The type of bargaining an employer and a majority union must engage in to meet their bargaining obligation under the Taft-Hartley Act. The parties are required to meet at reasonable times and to confer in good faith with respect to wages, hours, and other terms and conditions of employment. But neither party is required to agree to a proposal or to make a concession.

Grievance An employee complaint; an allegation by an employee, union, or employer that a collective bargaining contract has been violated.

Grievance committee Committee designated by a union to meet periodically with the management to discuss grievances that have accumulated.

Guard Plant protection employee. May not be represented by union affiliated with union of production employees under Taft-Hartley Act.

Hiring hall Place where workers are recruited for ships or waterfront activities or for work on construction projects.

Homework Piecework performed by workers in their own homes.

Hot goods Term applied by union members to products of plants employing strikebreakers, nonunion workers, or other workers regarded as hostile by union. Hot-goods or hot-cargo clauses under which a union gets an employer to agree not to require his employees to handle or work on hot goods or cargo were outlawed by one of the 1959 amendments to the Taft-Hartley Act.

Immunity clause Clause in a contract designed to protect a union from suits for contract violation growing out of unauthorized strikes. A typical clause would limit recourse of the parties to the grievance procedure of the contract.

Impartial umpire Person designated by agreement between a union and an employer or association of employers whose duty it is to arbitrate grievances or controversies arising under a contract.

Independent union Local labor organization not affiliated with a national organized union; union not affiliated with a national federation of unions.

Individual contract Agreement of employer with individual employee covering conditions of work.

Industrial union Labor organization admitting to membership all persons employed in a plant or industry, regardless of kind of work performed.

Industrial unit Bargaining unit composed of all production and maintenance workers in one or more plants, irrespective of the type of work done.

Informational picketing Picketing for the purpose of advising the public, including other union members, that the picketed employer does not have a union contract or is selling goods produced by a struck or nonunion employer. The 1959 amendments to the Taft-Hartley Act placed restrictions on such picketing.

Initiation fees Fees required by unions as a condition to the privilege of becoming members. If such fees are excessive or discriminatory, an employer may not be held to the obligation under a union shop of discharging employees who do not join the union.

Injunction Mandatory order by a court to perform or cease a specified activity usually on the ground that otherwise the complaining party will suffer irreparable injury from unlawful actions of the other party.

Inside union Plant union without outside affiliation.

Interference Short-cut expression for "interference with the right of employees to self-organization and to bargain collectively."

International union Nationally organized union having locals in another country, usually Canada.

Intimidation Actual or implied threats to induce employees to refrain from joining or to join a labor organization; threats used in other aspects of labor controversies, such as in picketing.

Joint council Body established in some industries consisting of representatives of union and of employer association,

its purpose being the settlement of disputes arising under a contract; body representing several craft unions in a plant or plants acting as a unit in collective bargaining.

Judicial review Proceedings before courts for enforcement or setting aside of orders of labor relations boards. Review is limited to conclusions of law, excluding findings of fact unless these are unsupported by evidence.

Jurisdiction Right claimed by union to organize class of employees without competition from any other union; province within which any agency or court is authorized to act. See *Work jurisdiction*.

Jurisdictional dispute Controversy between two unions over the right to organize a given class or group of employees or to have members employed on a specific type of work.

Jurisdictional strike A strike called to compel an employer to assign work to one class or craft of employees rather than to another. This is an unfair labor practice under the Taft-Hartley Act and may bring the question as to proper work assignment to the Labor Board for final decision.

Kickback Return of a portion of wages paid, usually in pursuance of an undisclosed agreement with the person who hires the employee.

Labor contract Agreement entered into between an employer and an organization of employees covering wages, hours, and conditions of labor.

Labor dispute As used in Norris-LaGuardia Act, a controversy involving persons in the same occupations or having interest therein or who work for the same employer or employers or who are members of the same or an affiliated union.

Labor relations board Quasi-judicial agency set up under national or state labor relations acts whose duty it is to issue and adjudicate complaints alleging unfair labor practices, to require such practices to be stopped, and to certify bargaining agents for employees.

Layoff Dropping a worker temporarily from the payroll, usually during a period of slack work, the intention being to rehire him when he is needed.

Local Group of organized employees holding a charter from a national or international labor organization. A local is usually confined to union members in one plant or one small locality.

Lockout Closing down of a business as a form of economic pressure upon employees to enforce acceptance of employer's terms, or to prevent whipsawing where union bargains with an association of employers.

Lodge Term used in some labor organizations as the equivalent of local. See *Local*.

Loyal worker An employee who refuses to join outside labor organization or to participate in strike. Term used by employer.

Maintenance of membership Union-security agreement under which employees who are members of a union on specified date, or thereafter become members, are required to remain members during the term of the contract as a condition of employment.

Majority rule Rule that the representative chosen by the majority of employees in an appropriate unit shall be the exclusive bargaining agent for all the employees.

Make-whole order Order issued by the NLRB requiring an employer who has refused to bargain in good faith under the Taft-Hartley Act to reimburse the employees for increased wages and other benefits they would have obtained had the employer bargained in good faith. The legality of such an order is in dispute.

Management rights clause Collective bargaining contract clause that expressly reserves to management certain rights and specifies that the exercise of those rights shall not be subject to the grievance procedure or arbitration.

Mandatory injunction Term applied to injunctions that the NLRB General Counsel is required to seek in the case of alleged unfair practices involving secondary boycotts, secondary-recognition strikes, recognition or organizational picketing, or strikes to force an employer to ignore an NLRB certification. Injunction remains in effect pending decision by the NLRB on the merits of the case.

Mediation Offer of service to parties to a dispute as an equal friend of each; differs from conciliation in that mediator makes proposals for settlement of the dispute that have not been made by either party.

Mediation Service Short form for Federal Mediation and Conciliation Service, which has a functional part in settlement of disputes under the Taft-Hartley Act.

Militarized guard Plant guard under authority of armed services in factories where work is being done under contract

with armed services. Militarized guards are on payroll of factory.

Moonlighting Practice of holding down two or more jobs at once, the second one usually being on a night shift.

Multiple employer unit Bargaining unit consisting of all production and maintenance workers employed by more than one employer.

Multiple plant unit Bargaining unit consisting of all production and maintenance workers in two or more plants among a larger number owned by one employer.

National Mediation Board Agency set up under the Railway Labor Act to mediate in case of labor disputes in railroad and air transport industry and to conduct elections for choice of bargaining agents.

National Railroad Adjustment Board Agency set up under the Railway Labor Act to settle disputes in railroad industry arising out of grievances or application of contracts.

Negotiating committee Committee of a union or an employer selected to negotiate a collective bargaining contract.

Open shop Plant where employees are declared by the employer to be free to join or not join any union; the opposite number to union or closed shop.

Organizational picketing Picketing of an employer in an attempt to induce the employees to join the union.

Outlawed strike Strike forbidden by law. See *Unauthorized strike.*

Outside union Nationally organized union seeking to organize workers in a plant previously unorganized or organized in a plant union.

Overtime Period worked in excess of a standard workday or workweek, for which time a wage rate above the standard is usually paid; money received for overtime work.

Paper jurisdiction Claim of a union to organizational rights over a certain class of employees when actually no attempt has been made to organize them.

Paper local A local union issued a charter by the parent organization before any members have been enrolled in the local. Paper locals figured in a joint board election investigated by the McClellan Committee, the votes of the paper locals having been used to swing the election.

Picketing Advertising, usually by members of a union carrying signs, the existence of a labor dispute and the union's version of its merits.

Piecework Work done for wages based on output rather than on time spent.

Plant union Organization of employees confined to one plant or factory.

Plant unit Bargaining unit consisting of all production and maintenance workers in a plant regardless of type of work performed.

Political expenditures The money spent by unions or corporations in connection with the nomination or election of federal officials. Such expenditures formerly were governed by the Federal Corrupt Practices Act and now are subject to the Federal Election Campaign Act (2 U.S.C. § 441(b)).

Preferential shop Arrangement with a union under which employer agrees to give certain preferences to union members in the matter of hiring or to require that a certain proportion of employees be members of the union.

Professional employee Employees qualifying as "professional" under Section 2(12) of the Taft-Hartley Act. They may not be included in a unit containing nonprofessional employees unless they so elect.

Publicity picketing Another term for picketing aimed at publicizing a labor dispute. See *Informational picketing.*

Racketeer Union official who uses his position to extort money from employers, usually by threatening to cause a strike.

Rank and file Members of a union other than the officers.

Recognition Acknowledging a union as bargaining agent for employees, either for all or only for those who are members of the union.

Recognition picketing Picketing for the object of inducing or compelling the employer to recognize the union as bargaining agent for the employer's employees. Recognition picketing conducted under certain circumstances was made an unfair labor practice by the 1959 amendments to the Taft-Hartley Act.

Referendum Special election under some state laws in which employees are polled on question whether they wish to authorize their bargaining agent to sign a union-security contract or to rescind such authority previously granted.

Regional director Official of the National Labor Relations Board who acts for the Board in a specified region.

Reinstatement Return to employment of persons unlawfully discharged.

Remedial order See *Affirmative order*.

Representation election See *Employee election*.

Restraint and coercion Term used in Section 8(b)(1) of Taft-Hartley Act making it an unfair labor practice for a union to restrain or coerce employees in the exercise of their rights to join unions or to engage in union activities or in the exercise of their rights to refrain from joining unions or engaging in such activities.

Right to work A term used to describe laws which ban union-security agreements by forbidding contracts making employment conditional on membership or nonmembership in labor organizations.

Run-away shop Plant moved by employer to avoid bargaining with a union representing his employees.

Run-off election Second employee election directed by a labor board when the first fails to show more than half the votes recorded for any one choice presented.

Sabotage Malicious damage done by employee to employer's equipment or other property.

Scab Epithet applied to non-striking employee by fellow employees on strike, carrying significance of "traitor."

Secondary boycott Refusal to deal with or buy goods from a concern which is the customer or supplier of an employer with whom the boycotters have a dispute. An indirect pressure is thus brought upon the primary object of the boycott.

Secondary strike A strike against an employer to force him to use pressure upon another employer, usually a supplier or customer, to induce the other employer to accede to demands of the union upon him.

Self-organization Self-determined activity by employees in the formation of labor unions.

Seniority Length of service with an employer or in one branch of a business; preference accorded employees on the basis of length of service.

Settlement agreement The terms agreed upon in the settlement of charges before the NLRB without a full-dress hearing, decision, and order. To be binding, such agreements must have the consent of the NLRB.

Share-the-work plan An arrangement under which, in lieu of cutting payroll when work falls off, the hours worked by each employee are shortened.

Shop steward Person designated by a union to take up with the foreman or supervisor the grievances of fellow employees as they arise.

Shop unit Subdivision of a union consisting of members employed in a single shop. Its affairs are ordinarily subject to decisions by a local. See *Local*.

Showing of interest Support union must show among employees in bargaining unit before NLRB will process union's election petition. The Board requires a union that is seeking a representation election to make a showing of interest among 30 percent of the employees in the bargaining unit.

Shutdown Temporary closing of plant, usually because of slack work or for changing plant equipment.

Sit-down strike Stoppage of work where the strikers remain in occupancy of the employer's premises.

Slowdown Concerted slackening of pace in working as a means of enforcing demands made by employees.

Soldiering Deliberate slackening of pace in work, usually as a protest against uncorrected grievances.

Speed-up Quickening the pace of operations performed by employees, usually through stepping up the speed of machines which they attend.

Statute of limitations As applied to unfair labor practices, a provision of the Taft-Hartley Act under which charges are outlawed if based on events more than six months old.

Stranger picketing Picketing conducted by persons who are not employees of the picketed employer. It has been held unlawful under the laws of some states.

Stretch-out Increasing work quota of employees, usually by increasing number of operations to be performed or of machines to be watched.

Strike Concerted cessation of work as a form of economic pressure by employees, usually organized, to enforce acceptance of their terms.

Strikebreaker One whose trade it is to take employment in struck plants. Distinguishable from "scab," who is a workman. May pretend to work in the plant or act as a guard.

Strike vote Balloting or canvass on question of calling a strike.

Struck work Work performed by employees of one employer that would have been performed by employees of another employer had they not been on strike.

Subcontracting Farming out of part of a plant's work to another company. Such diversion of work for the purpose of avoiding or evading the duty to bargain with a union is an unfair labor prac-

tice under the Taft-Hartley Act.

Superseniority Seniority granted by contract to certain classes of employees in excess of that which length of service would justify and which is protected against reduction by events which would have the effect of reducing seniority of other employees. Union stewards and veterans are sometimes accorded superseniority. The granting of superseniority to strikers' replacements has been held to be an unfair labor practice.

Supervisor An employee with authority to hire and fire or make effective recommendations to this effect. Supervisors enjoy no protection of bargaining rights under the Taft-Hartley Act.

Supplemental unemployment benefits Employer-financed payments to laid-off employees to supplement the state unemployment benefits they receive.

Surveillance Keeping watch on employees to detect evidence of union activity.

Sympathetic strike Strike called for the purpose of influencing outcome of a dispute in another enterprise or industry.

Unauthorized strike A strike by employees contrary to the advice or without the consent of their union.

Unemployment compensation System of federal and state law and taxation developed to provide emergency income to workers during periods of unemployment.

Unfair employment practice Discrimination in employment based on race, color, religion, sex, or national origin. Forbidden by federal and some state laws.

Unfair labor practice Practice forbidden by the national and several state labor relations acts.

Unfair labor practice strike Strike caused or prolonged in whole or in part by the employer's unfair labor practices. In such a strike, the employer must reinstate the strikers in their jobs, upon unconditional application, even though it is necessary to let replacements go.

Unfair list Names of employers publicized by unions as "unfair" because of their refusal to recognize the union or because of some other dispute.

Union Labor organization.

Union affiliation election Election in which members of a union decide if they want their union to become affiliated with another labor organization. Nonmembers of the union in the bargaining unit do not have to vote in such an election.

Union hiring System under which new employees must be chosen from among union members, the union determining the members to be taken on.

Union insignia Buttons or other signs worn by employees to indicate that they are union members. Prohibition against their display has been held unlawful interference with organizational rights, absent unusual circumstances.

Union label Marks placed on goods indicating that they have been made in a shop which deals with a labor union.

Union shop Arrangement with a union by which employer may hire any employee, union or nonunion, but the new employee must join the union within a specified time and remain a member in good standing.

Unit Shortened form of "unit appropriate for collective bargaining." It consists of all employees entitled to select a single agent to represent them in bargaining collectively.

Walkout Strike in which workers leave the shop or plant.

Welfare plan Arrangements with a union under which insurance and other benefits will be paid to employees and their families. Employer contributions are forbidden except under conditions laid down in Section 302 of the Taft-Hartley Act.

Whistleblowing Disclosure of improper employer practices or policies, such as defective products, corruption, or cost overruns. A number of federal and state laws protect whistleblowing employees from retaliation. Even without a specific law, some courts have held that whistleblowers may be protected by the First Amendment or by public policy considerations.

Wildcat strike An unauthorized strike. See *Outlawed strike*.

Work jurisdiction Right claimed by union under its charter to have its members and no others engaged in certain work. See *Jurisdictional dispute, Jurisdictional strike*.

Work permit Card issued by union having closed shop to show permission that holder, though not a full-fledged union member, may be employed under contract.

Yellow-dog contract Agreement under which an employee undertakes not to join a union while working for his employer.

Zipper clause Clause that seeks to close all employment terms for the duration of the labor contract by stating that the agreement is "complete in itself" and "sets forth all terms and conditions" of the agreement.

TABLE OF CASES

E

East Bay Newspapers, Inc., 225 NLRB 1148, 93 LRRM 1102 (1976) 25

East Dayton Tool & Die Co., 239 NLRB 141, 99 LRRM 1499 (1978) 72

Electrical Workers (IBEW)

—289 NLRB No. 81, 128 LRRM 1233 (1988)   27

—see Florida Power & Light Co. v.

—v. Foust, 442 US 42, 101 LRRM 2365 (1979)   77

—v. Hechler, 481 US —, 125 LRRM 2353 (1987) 16

—Local 3, 144 NLRB 5, 53 LRRM 1508 (1963), enf'd, 339 F2d 600, 58 LRRM 2095 (CA 2, 1964) 91

—Local 204, see Iowa Electric Light & Power v.

—Local 340; NLRB v., — US —, 125 LRRM 2305 (1987) 153

—Local 388; NLRB v., 548 F2d 704, 94 LRRM 2536 (CA 7), cert. denied, 434 US 837, 96 LRRM 2514 (1977) 115

—Local 400 (County of Ocean), 269 NLRB 119, 116 LRRM 1477 (1984) 96

—Local 474 v. NLRB, 814 F2d 697, 124 LRRM 2993 (CA DC, 1987) 47

—Local 494, see Boxhorn's Big Muskego Gun Club v.

—Local 497 (Apple City Elec.), 275 NLRB No. 176, 120 LRRM 1045 (1985) 74

—Local 501 v. NLRB (Pond Elec. Serv.), 756 F2d 888, 118 LRRM 3103 (CA DC, 1985)   98

—Local 803 v. NLRB, 826 F2d 1283, 126 LRRM 2065 (CA 3, 1987) 105

—Local 1395 v. NLRB, 797 F2d 1027, 122 LRRM 3265 (CA DC, 1986) 105

—Local 1464 (Kansas City Power & Light Co.), 275 NLRB No. 80, 119 LRRM 1147, supplemented, 275 NLRB No. 219, 120 LRRM 1057 (1985) 64

—Local 1547, see Stelling v.

—Local 1969, see Bise v.

—v. NLRB, 557 F2d 995, 95 LRRM 2996 (CA 2, 1977) 66

—see Ross v.

Electrical Workers (IUE)

—Local 459; NLRB v., 228 F2d 553, 37 LRRM 2219 (CA 2, 1955) 98

—Local 761 v. NLRB, 366 US 667, 48 LRRM 2210 (1961) 97

—Local 790 v. Robbins & Myers, Inc., 429 US 299, 13 FEP Cases 1813 (1976) 120

—v. NLRB, 426 F2d 1243, 73 LRRM 2870 (CA DC, 1970) 78

—v. NLRB, see Westinghouse Elec. Corp.

Elk Lumber Co., 91 NLRB 333, 26 LRRM 1493 (1950) 103

Elson Bottling Co.; NLRB v., 379 F2d 223, 65 LRRM 2673 (CA 6, 1967) 37

Emporium Capwell Co. v. Western Addition Community Org., 420 US 50, 88 LRRM 2660, 9 FEP Cases 195 (1975)   110

Erie Resistor Corp.; NLRB v., 373 US 221, 53 LRRM 2121 (1963) 30, 102

Ewing v. NLRB, 861 F2d 353, 129 LRRM 2853 (CA 2, 1988) 29

Ex-Cell-O Corp., 185 NLRB 107, 74 LRRM 1740 (1970), enf'd, 449 F2d 1058, 77 LRRM 2547 (CA DC, 1971) 78

Excelsior Underwear, Inc., 156 NLRB 1236, 61 LRRM 1217 (1966) 49

Exchange Parts Co.; NLRB v., 375 US 405, 55 LRRM 2098 (1964) 28

F

Fafnir Bearing Co., 146 NLRB 1582, 56 LRRM 1108 (1946), enf'd, 362 F2d 716, 62 LRRM 2415 (CA 2, 1966) 69

Fairmont Hotel, 282 NLRB No. 7, 123 LRRM 1257 (1986) 111

Fall River Dyeing & Finishing Corp. v. NLRB, — US —, 125 LRRM 2441 (1987)   77

Falmouth Co., 115 NLRB 1533, 38 LRRM 1124 (1956) 50

Fansteel Metallurgical Corp.; NLRB v. 306 US 240, 4 LRRM 515 (1939) 103

Farmer v. Carpenters Local 25, 430 US 290, 94 LRRM 2759 (1977) 133

Fibreboard Paper Prods. Corp. v. NLRB, 379 US 203, 57 LRRM 2609 (1964) 62

Filmation Assocs., 227 NLRB 1721, 94 LRRM 1470 (1977) 119

Financial Institution Employees (Seattle-First National Bank); NLRB v., 471 US 1098, 121 LRRM 2741 (1986) 154

Finnegan v. Leu, 456 US 431, 110 LRRM 2321 (1982) 133

First Nat'l Maintenance Corp. v. NLRB, 452 US 666, 107 LRRM 2705 (1981) 62

Y

INDEX

(See also Glossary of Labor Terms, p. 163)